DON RAMSEY

HORSE SENSE
101

21ST CENTURY
PRESS

WWW.21STCENTURYPRESS.COM

HORSE SENSE
101
"Using Common Sense to Lead Others"

Copyright © 2005
Donald L. Ramsey

Published by 21st Century Press
2131 W. Republic Rd.
PMB 41
Springfield, MO 65807

Scripture quotations are from the King James Version.

For more information about 21st Century Press visit our web site: www.21stcenturypress.com

ISBN 0-9749811-9-2

Cover Design: Keith Locke
Book Design: Terry White
Line Drawing: Jerry Ramsey

21ST CENTURY
PRESS
PUBLISHING WITH PURPOSE
WWW.21STCENTURYPRESS.COM

Comment

It doesn't matter how you hang your horseshoe! Successful leadership is by design, not luck. Your luck will have run out long before you begin…If you fail to exercise common sense.

"Wisdom
does not consist so much
in knowing what to do,
as in knowing what not to do
when you are ignorant;
the chief fault of the unwise
is driving toward conclusions
from insufficient premises."
—Sydney Harris

"The
wisdom of the wise
and the
experience of the ages
are perpetuated
by quotations."
—Benjamin Disraeli

To my friends
Diane & Steve —

This book is dedicated to my wife,
Shirley, my companion and confidant in life,
who provided the encouragement and support
to make this work possible.

Table of Contents

PREFACE

"Horse Sense" is an expression used to identify a demonstration of wisdom we acknowledge as common sense. My generation experienced the application of common sense principles. As a teen, I was exposed to reading, writing, arithmetic, and horse sense. Admonitions by parents and educators stressed the importance of exercising common sense. Common sense was reinforced at home as well as in the classroom. It was selectively used to teach, to discipline, to counsel, to rebuke, and to critique lifestyles or life choices.

Old fogy sayings, stories, and advice, often perceived to be "corny," were used to convey wisdom. These were packaged in cultural mores and passed along to succeeding generations. Each generation made relevant contributions to respond to life's realities. The principles espoused by these sayings are primitive, yet profound. They are profound, due to the fact they seem to be revelations of our attempt to conform to, and understand, divine principles, and the interaction of those principles with human nature. It is as if they are reflections that mirror a fundamental law or code of conduct. Perhaps they give us insight to practice truth.

Evidence of a perpetuated need for common sense directives is observed daily in our society. Common sense sayings, slogans, and wisdom vignettes are seen on everything from product advertisements to church marquees and bumper stickers. Os Guinness, in his insightful work entitled *Time for Truth,* refers to our generation as one that "dumbs down" everything to bumper stickers and Hallmark cards. I suspect "dumbing down" predates our generation and may have always been a prerequisite to insight.

Grandparents seemed to be more versed in common sense curriculum than parents. The generational reluctance to accept these principles was, to a degree, based on the fact they were perceived to be too simplistic. As a teenager I had difficulty believing my parents made it in life, apparently knowing so little. But a strange thing happened on the way to reality. The older I got, the wiser they became! The complexities of college, marriage, children, and debt dictated an urgent need for wisdom. After all, my parents had said, "Experience is always the best teacher."

Even the importance of an education was stressed with such parental reminders. Pungent messages were cloaked in simplicity: "What you put in your head no one will ever take from you." and "It's better to use your head than it is your back to earn a living." I am sure these admonitions contributed to my academic interests. Upon completion of some of my academic work and egotistically progressing beyond the simplicities of common sense, I was given a reality check. I was reminded by a sage that a degree is like the curl in a pig's tail, it may make the pig look good but it doesn't change the taste of the pork. I was fortunate to learn that academic achievement without common sense is like a boat without an oar. You may be afloat in the water but you won't go far without it. Academic knowledge void of common sense is best described by the insightful observations of a former college president acquaintance. After serving for years in academic work, he concluded, "Some people are educated beyond their intelligence."

> "One pound of learning requires ten pounds of common sense to apply it."
>
> —Anonymous

Common sense is perhaps the most frequently identified need in life. In fact, the ability to interact with life requires it. It is referenced in the home, at school, in the work place, and even in legal matters. Success in business, in marital relations, and in personal interactions is predicated on our ability to exercise prudence. The leadership role demands that a leader exercise common sense. A successful leader will be sensitive to the personal need of "unsophisticated wisdom."

A Bibliocentric truth reminds us, "There is nothing new under the sun." Since wisdom is ageless, "All that is past is preface."

Disclosure…

Truth is under siege! Truth as an absolute is no longer an axiom. It is questioned, belittled, ridiculed, ignored, and perverted. A denial of truth allows every person to do that which is right in their own eyes. Socially constructed truth, or truth independent of divine authority is birthed in selfishness and nurtured by ego. There is no criteria for right or wrong. It spawns an environment ripe for anarchy.

I acknowledge my bias. I prefer to call it conviction, but this term may be foreign to some readers. I accept without reservation the credibility of the Bible as a sacred message that espouses divine principles. I also embrace the exclusivity of its authority for rule and practice without apology. This persuasion is rooted in the belief that all truth finds its origin in the divine. The reader will be advised to understand this perspective in researching with me the value of common sense. I furthermore challenge the reader to explore this premise as a possibility for his or her own enrichment.

"The

truth

shall make you free,

but first

it shall make you

miserable."

—Barry Stevens

"Men occasionally

stumble over the

truth, but most

of them pick

themselves up and

hurry off as if

nothing has

happened."

—Winston Churchill

INTRODUCTION

The focus of this work is to assess and explore the potential of common sense in the leadership role. In an attempt to do justice to the subject it was necessary to quantify the essence of common sense. Common sense, also identified as "HORSE SENSE," is based on a basic principle of truth.

Common sense is the demonstrated affirmation of an individual's sensitivity to a knowledge base derived from truth principles. These principles have found expression in folk wisdom, parabolic expressions, allegories, recited sayings, and even "pop psychology." It is rooted in life experiences and transcends cultural traditions. Simplicity facilitates understanding, and appears to have contributed to its perpetuation. More often than not, "common sense" expressions of truth are unsophisticated, and in some cases perceived to be crude.

Often these sayings and slogans of homespun wisdom are given sacred status. Heated arguments have contested their origin and many are persuaded they are Biblical quotes. I suppose this could be an indication of the depth of their roots. Due to the religious traditions from which our values emerged, they are a part of the very fiber of our society. Certainly, a principle, if true, is of divine origin even if there is no chapter and verse reference.

Frequent reminders of a time when, "A man's word was his bond," reverberate from the past. Previous generations are quick to remind us that a handshake in their generation was more binding, contractually, than any legal document. My father recited to me on numerous occasions, "A man that will lie to you will steal from you." Truth was the heartbeat of this common sense approach to life. These oft repeated sayings seemed to have originated from sensitivity to truth and error. Intuitively, this sensitivity seemed to sort out error and embrace truth. Perhaps this explains the dynamics that made these sayings so forceful and enduring.

Truth embellished is truth lost. Truth experienced is truth affirmed. Truth expressed is truth learned. Truth embraced is knowledge gained. Truth does not change. Circumstances change, situations change, and interpretations may be susceptible to error or, in some cases, be self-serving, but the principle of truth is unalterable. Truth is not new, it is divine and it is eternal.

In this examination of common sense, I have merely plagiarized my life experience with truth as I have observed it in unsophisticated wisdom. I make no claim to originality. Experientially, the gleanings of tenured leadership roles provided reinforcement of a long embraced premise. Common sense is based on truth principles, and it is integral to true leadership. The failure to exercise common sense negates every good attribute of leadership. Leadership skills, personal charm, education, fiscal expertise, positive attitudes, and successful dress are short lived without the ability to exercise common sense. Enthusiastic individuals that are mesmerized by their own natural abilities and attributes will be the first to experience disenchantment when common sense is not exercised. Skilled leaders in responsible roles can, and do, overlook common sense principles.

Unlike previous generations, ours has had access to unlimited resources, educational publications, academic courses, and seminars on leadership development. Many have accessed these resources and discovered that their leadership effectiveness is as illusive as the proverbial needle in the haystack. Two glaring oversights are prevalent in our fast paced, enlightened, profit driven environment. The first is the lack of sensitivity to unsophisticated wisdom. The second is the assumption that all individuals in prominent leadership roles possess basic leadership skills. Both are the result of a wisdom deficit.

The focus of this work will, hopefully, inspire you to examine unsophisticated wisdom as a viable supplement to your formal preparation to be a leader. It is my desire that you, the reader, will discover a life changing dynamic for new horizons in leadership. Please understand the intent is not to critique others. The concepts proposed are the end result of personal experience and lessons learned from life. It is as much a personal introspection of, and musings of, my own life experience and/or mistakes as it is the observation of others. I have tried to make the discernment of manifested strengths and demonstrated mistakes my laboratory for learning. I have attempted to appreciate and value wisdom that has neither degree nor credentialed source.

An accepted misconception perceives age to be a pre-requisite for one to exercise common sense. Even though experience and age are motivations to pursue wisdom, neither are required. It is true that maturity seems to have a greater appreciation for common sense, while youth is tempted to stigmatize it. It has been suggested that when you've learned enough to lead, society dictates you're too old to lead. Imagine if you will, the composite potential of youth, zeal, talent, education, and common sense. For some, common sense is "a day late and a dollar short." "Timing is everything!"

"Obsolescence
too
quickly
follows
adolescence."
—Jack Kraus

"Wisdom
supports a sage
perspective on life,
a sense of balance,
a keen understanding
of how the various
parts and principles
apply and relate
to each other.

It embraces judgment,
discernment, comprehension.
It is oneness, an integrated
wholeness."
—Stephen Covey

CHAPTER 1

HORSE SENSE

Common sense has been vaunted, referenced, belittled, scorned, revered, and claimed. Regardless of one's response to it, the fact is all have contemplated its virtues and exercised it to a greater or lesser degree. The psyche appears to have a natural propensity to subscribe to the need of rational thinking. Either the use of it or the failure to use it imprints life-changing decisions. History is replete with the biographies of both. Every aspect of society is affected by its influence. Consequently, successive civilizations give evidence of a resourcefulness to access common sense.

Democracy in America was birthed in common sense. Thomas Payne's "Common Sense" pamphlet was a silent partner in the American Revolution accomplishing what the Continental Congress had been unable to do. The circulation of this forty-six-sheet document was unprecedented in that its dissemination spread through the colonies like a prairie fire. In a country of less than three million, 120,000 copies were sold in the first three months. Copies were circulated to friends, groups, and neighbors, making the distribution even more remarkable. It has been considered the best selling written work in American History. The forcefulness of truth presented in the vernacular of common sense silenced dissenters and convinced doubters, creating a demand for independence. The use of common sense distinguishes the outcome.

G.K. Chesterton acknowledged "common sense" as instinct for the probable. He was convinced the common sense of Aristotle made him perhaps the greatest of all philosophers, and if not, certainly the most practical.

Common sense, frequently called "Horse Sense," is defined as,

THE UNREFLECTIVE OPINIONS OF ORDINARY PEOPLE: SOUND AND PRUDENT, BUT OFTEN UNSOPHISTICATED JUDGEMENT.

Horse sense and common sense will be used interchangeably as we examine examples that parlay its forcefulness and research the potential it has for the leader and the leadership role.

The equestrian will have little difficulty with the use of the vernacularism. Some may choose to argue that the actions of a trained horse could never depict innate wisdom. We do know that horses can and do demonstrate a sensitivity and responsiveness to the obvious. So caution is urged for the skeptical.

Horse training techniques now being implemented identify triggers and conditioned responses to reduce transition stress. Much has been learned regarding the impact of familiarity, unfamiliarity, space, and fear in this training process. The empirical signs of readiness for change are being examined and considered as models for human motivation and change.

Untrained horses have a propensity for flight: man has a propensity to fight. Traditional horse training methods are now deemed counterproductive. Brute force used to bring horse behavior into submission only serves to traumatize the animal. New techniques employ gentleness to make the proximity of the animal to the trainer a safe zone for protection and nurture. When the animal understands nearness to the trainer is a good place and not a bad place, the horse will validate a relationship. There is now irrefutable evidence that wild horses demonstrate behavior modification within hours using a nonviolent training approach. Monty Roberts, horse trainer, concludes:

1. Horses don't forget anything.
2. Horses are capable of conscious thought.

The applicability of horse training to leadership extends far beyond the scope of our examination of the importance of horse sense. Suffice to say, perhaps a kinder, gentler approach should be seriously considered by the leader.

The term, as used in the context of our research, is to denote the ability of an individual to understand and take appropriate action based on simplistic interpretations of truth. Successful leaders are leaders that value simplicity. This book is written to stimulate leader sensitivity to this invaluable resource. The principles can be applied to any and all leadership roles. The title, or position, is irrelevant. Leadership role requirements for the politician, the corporate executive, or the minister, are all the same.

A conscious effort has been made to refrain from suggesting "packaged success" to leaders. Prescriptive concepts in a common sense format can provide insight but cannot guarantee success. Energized common sense can, and will, have a positive impact. Common sense is the resource most often overlooked by leaders who are committed to excellence in their leadership role. Common sense can be obscured by a preoccupation with the academics of leadership. The ability to comprehend common sense principles for daily living is a pre-requisite to understand the applicability of these truths to the leadership role.

In writing this book I was confronted with a thought provoking question, "Can horse sense be taught?" The answer must be found in additional probes. Can we trace its origin? Does it evolve and can it be perpetually relevant? Its importance is continually stressed in leadership seminars. Most written works on the subject of leadership development will make references to its value. The issue is, can we discipline ourselves to comprehend it? Perhaps common sense logic can even provide answers to these important questions.

An in-depth response to these questions and any preoccupation with a debate over contested possibilities is clearly not the focus of our attention. Answers to such questions could lead to a contentious debate without a resolution. This possibility would be a distraction, or distort the intent of the text. I do believe an assessment to determine the value of common sense truths will provide insight and direction for the attentive reader. I, personally, am persuaded that common sense is established upon truth principles. Truth can be taught. If common sense is the end result of a principle of truth, it can be learned. It is apparent that it evolves, can be perpetually relevant, and often is culturally specific.

Bumper stickers and marquees substantiate the existence of an evolutionary process. More recently, common sense is communicated through an array of simplistic sayings veiled in either humor or sarcasm. "Do unto others, then split!" and "The Golden Rule: He who has the gold makes the rules." are two classic examples that scornfully depict contemporary attitudes.

Some common sense sayings are used to portray diverse possibilities. The inability and futility of an attempt to make something out of nothing was captured by the common sense expression, "You can't make a purse out of a sow's ear." The concept has also been used to express one's ability to perform the unthinkable. "They made a purse out of a sow's ear." Horse sense is an attempt to simplify, define, comprehend, and convey truth.

It is Culturally Generic

Even though the expressions of common sense by diverse ethnic groups may be culturally personalized, truth is relative to all. The exclusivity of an expression often is a reflection of the culture, its values, and personalized struggles. Common sense reveals not only our diversity, but also our sameness. As members of the human race, we are all confronted with life changing choices and challenges that require common sense logic. A friend of mine, of differing ethnicity, often recites his mother's expressions of common sense truth. As a successful businessman, he still recalls his mother's wisdom regarding priorities she observed in his preferred life style. His love for expensive automobiles prompted her admonition, "Son, you should never ride higher than you live."

It is a Key to Success

The recognition of the value of common sense truth for daily living is undergraduate work for success. Astute leaders are constantly in pursuit of professional success. They attend every success seminar, leadership enrichment course, and read all the current literature on leadership skills development. Every resource is invaluable, and most resources provide innovative ideas to stimulate creativity. On occasions, these individuals are surprised by unexpected outcomes. "The Four Steps to Successful Leadership," or whatever the tantalizing title, doesn't always result in euphoric success when put into practice. The implied or promised outcome is elusive. It is important to remember that the best-marketed success secrets are of little benefit without a basic understanding of human nature. Acceptance of the premise of truth in common sense, and a basic understanding of human nature are imperative to successful leadership. The scorn of wisdom cloaked in unsophisticated language can be a costly oversight on the road to success. The humor of the label "corny" may be serious business.

It is a Training Tool

Common sense principles find expression in folk wisdom, parabolic expressions, and practical life experience applications. Christ was the greatest teacher that ever lived, and he used simplistic, every day stories to instruct his listeners. Lessons energizing logic were taught using the stability of a house built on a rock, as opposed to one built on the sand. Preparedness for the inevitability of the storm made the message more relevant. He spoke of customs related to the marriage ceremony to demonstrate a lack of wisdom in the un-preparedness of five of ten virgins. He taught using illustrations from nature and logic from life events. His lessons always applied truth principles to a person's basic needs. People hurt, they cry, they laugh, they're bad, and they're good. They have self-actualization needs, they need instruction, they need hope, they need to feel they are important, they need to feel they can make a difference, and they need to know they are valuable.

It Can be Uncomfortable

The preponderance of evidence supports the premise that common sense is predicated on truth principles. Truth can be disconcerting and uncomfortable. Truth may contradict accepted norms, but it will always produce the right results. Our society spurns absolutes for living. Today, truth is interpreted as situational. Truth is distorted by convenience, prosperity, and selfish motives. Truth is absolute regardless of circumstances or life events. All have sacrificed truth for self-gratification. Suffering minorities in American history found the strength to survive because they embraced truth. Our democracy was rooted in truth, "We hold these truths to be self evident." The information provided in this book is for the leader who values truth and desires to examine more closely its resourcefulness.

It Has Been a Quest

Humanity's history is a history of an unrelenting quest to gain knowledge. It is either motivated by self-serving motives or a sincere desire to gain the knowledge required to serve others. The pursuit of knowledge to discern truth will serve others. The pursuit of knowledge, without regard for truth, only serves selfish ambitions. Effective leadership serves those who are led.

Wisdom desired for personal gain emerged at the dawn of creation. The Biblical record reminds us that neither the wonder of creation nor the blissfulness of Eden prevented selfish pursuits and the peril of self-serving motives. In fact, the human race's obsession with knowledge initiated a course of action that squandered its divine endowments, determined its destiny, and ignored its benefactor. We are introduced in the Garden to the relentless ambitions of the human race to acquire knowledge. Eve, then Adam, zealously attempted an unlawful, self-serving intrusion into the forbidden wisdom of God. This quest for knowledge vividly reveals the disparity that now exists between the created and the Creator. A true quest for wisdom is not to be "all knowing." It is a motivational desire to understand knowledge.

It Has Divine Implications

The inability to comprehend truth is identified as a spiritual deficiency in the Bible.

I Corinthians 2:14

"But the natural man receiveth not the things of the Spirit of God: for they are foolishness unto him: neither can he know them, because they are spiritually discerned."

—King James Version

Without insight it is impossible to fathom evidentiary truth in the most basic examples of the life experience. An example of this is evidenced in the inability to demonstrate a comprehension of the popular "Golden Rule" principle; "Do unto others as you would have them do unto you." This rule predates Mosaic Law and is incompatible with the barbarism that prevailed in historical societies. It has been embraced by all religions as an inspirational touchstone.

The Biblical book of Proverbs is a primer on wisdom for life. It attempts to establish meaningful priorities for living. Insights to wisdom, understanding, and knowledge are the prevalent themes. An open minded, casual reading of the book will enrich the reader. The applicability of the principles espoused in the writing to the leadership role will positively impact the learning curve of leadership skill development. An example of common sense thinking is found in the twenty-fourth chapter of the book.

Proverbs 24:30-34

"I went by the field of the slothful, and by the vineyard of the man void of understanding; And, lo, it was grown over with thorns, and nettles had covered the face thereof, and the stone wall thereof was broken down. Then I saw and considered it well: I looked upon it, and received instruction. Yet a little sleep, a little slumber, a little folding of the hands to sleep: So shall thy poverty come as one that travaileth; and thy want as an armed man."

—King James Version

The passage clearly identifies the expected outcome of an individual who is "void of understanding." Common sense dictates that an unkempt vineyard will be unproductive and lead to poverty for the vineyard keeper. The book of Proverbs should be read by two people; the person who feels they know all there is to know about leadership, and the person who has already discovered how little they really know about the subject.

Credible leaders lead by example. The leader must do more than demonstrate the knowledge to plant a vineyard and dream of a harvest. A leader must demonstrate the ability to respond to and act upon reality. Reality dictates the obvious. A productive vineyard requires attentive ownership and the active work of a keeper.

Leaders mesmerized by their own success and obsessed with recognition or fame can be vulnerable to the obvious. Leaders who deny reality, or create their own perception of reality, can easily overlook the needs of an unattended vineyard. The lack of attention to an obvious outgrowth of weeds and thorns, or the denial that they exist, will prevent a plentiful harvest.

"Life is not a bed of roses," and care for the rose bed requires respect for the thorns. The sweet smell of roses is only enjoyed when the gardener is not oblivious to the care of the garden. This requires a leader who will value painful truth, while focusing on the beauty of it. If leadership is credible, it must exemplify truth. If successful, it must be credible. A prominent Christian leader and college president often reminded students, "The success of any organization rises or falls on leadership."

It is a Challenge

It is one thing to have expertise and initiative to reach noble goals. It is quite another to motivate those you lead to mutually capture your vision. A delusionary façade is a "time capsule" for failure.

"YOU CAN LEAD A HORSE TO WATER BUT YOU CAN'T MAKE HIM DRINK."

...LEADERSHIP IS MORE THAN LEADING THE HORSE TO WATER...

LEADERSHIP IS GETTING THE HORSE TO DRINK!

In the following pages we will examine practical processes and "Horse Sense" thinking to accomplish this end.

"The
most important single
ingredient
to the formula
of success
is
knowing how
to get along
with
people."
—Teddy Roosevelt

CHAPTER 2

PEOPLE BUSINESS

If you are a leader...you are in the "PEOPLE BUSINESS!" A leader must be a "people person," one who likes people, enjoys their company, and can relate to them on their terms. More than being in the "PEOPLE BUSINESS" you are in the "PEOPLE BUILDING BUSINESS." I recently observed a freight carrier's motto on a passing eighteen-wheeler truck that stated, "Our driving force is people." This slogan captures the leader's mandate.

> "A leader who develops people, adds. A leader who develops leaders, multiples."
>
> —John Maxwell

"If you help people succeed, they will make you successful." The Divine principle of doing unto others as you would have them do unto you is a truth so priceless, its name depicts its worth. We call it the "Golden Rule." Wisdom's source is truth and cannot be attributed to our own innate ability. Ego driven ingenuity plagiarizes truth and claims originality. Truth dictates for us the rules of engagement and governs our interaction with others.

Three Stumbling Blocks

Egotistical traits, incompetence, and the lack of credibility impedes, if not prevents, "People Building." The leader, by virtue of position and role, has gained a degree of notoriety. An obsession with notoriety can lead to career ending behaviors. Attention to credibility and due diligence to competence are equally important. A recurring theme of three stumbling blocks emerges in this book. Ego, competency, and credibility loom large to the centrality of our subject.

A Spiritual Dimension

There is a spiritual dimension to leadership. Individuals are spiritual beings. Spiritual beings represent worth. The acceptance and acknowledgement of this fact prevents abusive behavior, or barbaric acts, and determines the value we place on people.

An unwritten law of conversational etiquette has forbidden open discussion of religion in our society. Political correctness and selective interpretations of the public role of spirituality by the vocal few have consigned faith traditions to the closet. Religion or faith expressions are tabooed based on the argument, "some may find it offensive." Individuals who use vulgarity, slang, or make condescending remarks about religion and religious practices are exempt from the same social mores. Typically, faith traditions are left in the pew of the church sanctuary or in the synagogue as the individual makes their departure from their place of worship. The closing of the hymnal, prayer book, or Bible places their faith on hold until the same time, same station, next worship service. This is true even of those most devoted to their faith traditions.

In crisis, the same general public will unashamedly invoke divine intervention. Survivors, politicians, and athletes have no difficulty expressing faith, even under the scrutiny of the national media, when emotionally overcome with gratitude or competitive ambition. A faith tradition for the majority of individuals is perceived to be little more than a fire escape or a lucky rabbit's foot. Leaders should come out of the closet with their faith traditions and access this tested dynamic for personal strength and effective leadership. We choose to wear either a spiritual hat or a secular hat, but fail to realize one size fits all.

Worldly things, or things not regarded as sacred are considered to be secular. Secularism is a system of political or social philosophy that rejects all forms of religious faith and worship. The denotation of a secular life is a misnomer for the individual identified as a Christian. The dichotomy of compartmentalizing life as either secular or Christian is dysfunctional for the professing Christian. Your value system is based on what you believe. What you believe defines who you are. Who you are is more important than what you are. Who you are is neither a persona or hat change. Secularism is more popular and more comfortable due to our personal struggles with spirituality and truth. The fact is, as living mortals, we are spiritual beings. Our distinction between the secular and sacred robs us of spiritual insight to truth. The nurturing impact of the recognition of the spiritual dimension will provide the proper soil for rapid growth.

My emphasis on the spiritual dimension is not to be misconstrued as an endorsement of the philosophical and meditative exercises of eastern religions. In recent years there has been a tendency for corporations to introduce and sometimes mandate these spiritual exercises in the work place to enhance productivity and stimulate work place morale. Philosophically, these practices are more often than not a contradiction to Biblio-centric faith traditions. The experiential adherence to biblical principles negates the need for supplemental sources of inspiration. Likewise, any emphasis on the spiritual dimension should never be seized by the opportunistic zealot to proselytize converts. Any and all faith traditions must be respected, but none should be imposed on subordinates.

An Example, Not An Exclamation Mark

Build by example, not declaration. Exemplify, don't indoctrinate! Embrace and practice the truth principles of your personal faith, and allow the power of truth to speak for itself. The recognition of, and the practice of truth in your faith tradition is not a license to impose dogma or doctrine on co-workers in the workplace. Practice; don't preach! Stay focused on the principles that value people. The truth of your tradition does not license you to be obnoxious or a nuisance. Respect truth in the faith tradition of others.

"We teach what we know, but reproduce what we are."

—John Maxwell

Growth Through Fun

Laborious and stressful work can be performed in a fun environment, if the leader can overcome his or her preoccupation with success. A leader obsessed with self, position, fame, acclaim, or egocentric success will project an image that inhibits growth and stifles fun. Happy workers are productive workers! Productive workers grow! Employees that enjoy their work environment will enjoy their work. Create an environment for growth.

Plants need the rain, but they also need sunshine. "Gloom, despair, and agony on me," should be relegated to the late '60s, early '70s television series "HEE HAW." The opportunity for fun should be allowed free expression. Individuals that enjoy their work and their work environment will blossom. Demanding schedules, productivity quotas, and the bottom line create an atmosphere of stress. Fun eases stress. The age of technology increases the demands made on the average employee. The utopian projections for the electronic age are only myths. Less work in fewer hours with greater productivity has not materialized. The average worker's time commitments alone emphasize the need to make the work place an enjoyable experience. Calculate the waking hours a person either spends at work, the commute to work, or related preoccupations with work events. Few, if any, would have a time commitment of only forty hours. Sleep alone consumes approximately forty-nine hours a week. Conservative calculations reveal the average individual has less than seventy-nine hours a week to shop, participate in worship, attend to family obligations, mow grass, clean house, do the laundry, and socialize. It is easy to see, few hours remain for a person to recreate.

Fun requires more than lip service; it demands a leader's commitment. The leader that either considers fun to be objectionable or masquerades participating approval will be victimized by their own selfish intentions. If objectionable, expect low morale and less productivity. If a masquerade, expect exercises to be scorned and short lived. Celebrations of fun must be free of self-serving motives designed to focus attention on the leader. Superficiality or hypocrisy will be interpreted as "the same old song and dance." Fun that energizes is natural and spontaneous.

People Building Philosophy

Value People

People building skills will be examined more carefully later. Now I want to focus on the philosophy that drives a "people building" initiative. Our philosophy effects our overall vision or attitude toward life and the purpose of life. The greatest challenge of any leader, or organization, is "building people," but the motive must be right. All manufacturers produce a product, but not all manufacturers produce a serviceable product. The difference is determined by motivation. A self examination exercise could be beneficial to assess motivation. Is it selfish or selfless? Is it designed to embellish the chief executive's finances; or is it designed to build the organization? Is it short term or long term? Is it for personal recognition; or truly recognition of staff? Does it build your ego as a leader; or does it build the staff and your organization?

In large corporations stockholders and boards are often a factor in the equation, and can negatively impact the quality of a product by demands for immediate profit at any cost. Short-term, career focused executives are always more concerned with the bottom line than they are the product. Those that manufacture inferior products are driven by greed or self-centered motives. Product quality is often sacrificed for profit and recognition. Don't lose sight of the fact: quality people build quality products. Quality people will build you an exemplary organization. Invest your life in something that will outlast you. Your investment will reap big dividends.

Organizations and stockholders are now identifying the quality of their people as an intangible asset. People are an organization's most valuable asset, and "people building" its greatest challenge. The issue is value. Do you value people as persons; or as self-serving commodities? Any pretense to "build people" must exemplify truth. The people you lead will quickly discern truth. Unrealistic expectations, unbearable work assignments, manipulative leadership policies, and failure to follow through with financial rewards quickly reveal a leader's real motivation.

Study People

People are basically the same. They have the same fears, hopes, dreams, and disappointments. People's actions and reactions demonstrate predictable patterns of behavior. Become a student! Study people. Study their friendships, associations, and reactions. Discipline yourself to be attentive in the classroom of life.

Every life is a story. Our perceptions are limited to restricted observations. Perceptions can be misleading and may be your downfall unless you take the time to understand the actions that created the perception. A person's real story is shaped by who they are, what they have experienced, where they have been, and what is going on in their life. Insights into these areas require time, empathy, and patience. Knowledge has a way of changing perceptions and actions.

When I was in pastoral work, I often jokingly cautioned parents to be sensitive to any negative remarks regarding pastoral leadership in the privacy of their homes because their children would tell on them. Busy little ears hear more than parents realize. Most pastoral leaders can relate to an occasion when a family left the parish, church, or synagogue, and a child demonstrated apprehension over any casual interaction with the pastoral leader due to negative discussions in their home environment. The innocence of a child's body language and demeanor is the best indicator of what parents really believe and say about others.

Be observant and listen more than you talk. Attention in this classroom requires a greater time commitment to listening than it does to talking. Learn to listen! Listen as intently to what is not said as to what is said. What is not said is usually more important. Our ability to learn is lost when we monopolize the conversation, so learn the art of self-discipline. If one learns the discipline of listening intently, it makes exam time more pleasant. Every leader, at some point in time, will be tested by the actions or conduct of those they lead. A good student is a disciplined student, so capitalize on your classroom time. The payoff will be worth it, and your report card will reveal it.

Your ability to lead is contingent on your knowledge base. You must observe every gesture and non-verbal communication. You must study people more diligently than you study leadership principles or techniques. It is imperative that you learn what makes people tick. Learn their body language, their subtle glances, and passing remarks. Understand, we all possess differing personality traits, and all, after being carefully studied, will demonstrate predictable behaviors. If you do your homework, you will discover you can have surprising success predicting unpredictable behaviors.

People Business

Good people with a vision build organizations. This criterion requires you to make people building your primary focus. Several factors that contribute to this realization include the right staff, with the right assignment, working in the right environment. This cannot be accomplished without a firm commitment to know and grow people.

People Are Important

Influence

"No person lives to himself or dies to himself" is a Biblical truth that stresses the significance of relationships. We are a part of something bigger than our own little world. We are, in a real sense, a part of every person we've ever met. Our persona cannot conceal the influence of our relationships with others. It appears we learn by osmosis.

"Everything that irritates us about others can lead us to an understanding of ourselves."

—Carl Jung

How often this is demonstrated in parent child relationships. The adult child realizes they are subconsciously demonstrating the same behavior they loathed in their parent. It is seen in children and long marriage relationships. It may be admiration, modeling, peer pressure, intimidation, competition, or some other imprimatur, but it happens. The explanations may differ, but the evidence is overwhelming. This happenstance stresses the importance of our relationship choices and makes everyone we meet an important component of all we hope to be. The value we attach to our relationships will reflect the value we place on people.

Ironies
"The people you pass on the way up, you will meet on your way down." Today's fast changing success oriented environment often results in unexpected ironies. Individuals you once supervised may at a later date become your supervisor. Leadership relationships established on trust and governed by a respect for others will prove to be the best insurance policy for future eventualities. People remember how they are treated and reciprocate accordingly. "What goes around comes around." Youthful subordinates that are highly qualified will often climb the success ladder more rapidly than those that hire them. Due to our fast paced computerized society, individuals are jokingly admonished to be kind to the "geeks" they meet today, because tomorrow these same "geeks" will control their destinies.

Disposable Commodities
We are a disposable society generating so much waste that it is becoming a major concern for most communities. This mentality appears to have influenced us philosophically. Capitalistic ambitions and prosperity have created a self-centered perspective on the values of life. The allurement of unprecedented wealth has caused organizations

and leaders to regard people as a disposable commodity. When the worth of a person is relegated to a line item on an annual budget, people will be perceived as disposable. Shortsighted obsessions with profit margins and aggressive career goals have caused leaders to focus on immediate gratification. Peer pressure, job security, and personal egos have fueled the fire. Actually, the most priceless commodity an organization possesses is the people who can make it happen.

Unscrupulous leaders perceive people as disposable commodities. This perception finds expression in the conscious choice to recycle people rather than adequately compensate them. These leaders leave a trail of casualties. People are more than a means to an end; they are caretakers of your organization's destiny. They have the capability to make you look better than you really are, or could ever hope to be. Whatever the motivation, this shortsightedness on the part of a leader, or an organization, will result in costly, long-term consequences.

Building people will prove to be your best investment. Build people and you will build profitable, productive organizations! "Don't get the cart before the horse!"

Integrity

People building demands substance. A leader without integrity is a shadow of the real thing. Chicanery cannot alter the vagueness of the image. You cannot follow or learn from an illusion. Integrity is more than an illusion. Integrity is defined as an uncompromising adherence to moral and ethical principles; soundness of moral character; honesty. Integrity, as is character, is who we are, not what we say we are. There is no such thing as "selective or convenient" integrity. You either have it or you don't. It can be costly and uncomfortable to some. It is the tenacity to act upon personalized, oral, and ethical principals that exemplify truth. Integrity doesn't differentiate between spoken or inferred commitments. It binds a person to their communication. If it does not, there is a character deficiency. Subterfuge is futile. An attempt to create an image of integrity through embellishment will be transparent. Excessive verbiage or misrepresentations only serve to exaggerate a flawed character. Integrity is evidentiary. Its aura cannot be duplicated or mimicked. Likewise, deceitfulness radiates, but its glow is a caustic contaminant.

It has been my experience that leadership style is inseparably linked to our philosophy on life. Our philosophy is a composite mixture of our character, mental and ethical values, life experiences, and culture. What we accept, excuse, or ignore as a leader reveals our value system. Examples are readily apparent. Individuals with disreputable backgrounds will be inclined to ignore the importance of historical honesty, and individuals with inadequate credentials or experience will overlook incompetence.

Using Influence for Financial Gain

Treasure your relationships. Guard them with your own integrity. Never misuse your position to coerce, intimidate, or persuade people to become involved in self-centered pursuits, whether for personal profit, a search for identity, or spirituality. Mutual respect is the issue. You have an awesome responsibility to respect the integrity of all you lead, and your ability to lead is determined by the respect subordinates have for you. If you have gained their respect, you gained it by the qualities they observe in your life. Respect is earned, not self-promoted. The respect you have earned should never be for sale. If it is, you sell your self-respect, and it is priceless.

Opportunists will solicit your influence and ability to motivate people for their own personal gain. Don't allow unscrupulous individuals to market your leadership skills for their products, programs, or philosophies. The scope may range from merchandising products, to pyramid schemes, to marketable utopian life styles. In response to temptations to merchandise successful leadership skills, leaders must ask of themselves probing questions. Is the motive personal enrichment or financial profit? Are the recruiters interested in me, or, are they interested in what I can do for them?

Get rich schemes at the expense of others will prove to be, personally, costly. Alluring enticements to misuse relationships are costly. Not only will you jeopardize your relationships, but you will also have your attention diverted from your leadership role. It will distract you from the focus that generated your success. An inability to stay focused on your organization's mission is a precursor to instability. Instability leads to confusion, and confusion ends in failure. A Biblical principle dealing with a person's life pursuits reminds us, "A double minded man is unstable in all his ways."

First Impressions

"First impressions are lasting impressions." This is true. It is not true that they are always correct! It does emphasize the importance of making individuals feel important at the point of the initial contact. Success with first encounters develops meaningful relationships. At the initial point of contact, your actions, demeanor, appearance, and conversation speak loudly.

One of two messages will be communicated in first encounters. The message will either be, "I am important," or "You are important." If the message communicated makes you important and your new acquaintance inferior, the foundation of any desired relationship is already flawed. One side note to remember is the importance of a person's name in first encounters. It has been suggested that nothing is sweeter to an individual than the sound of their own name. The following quote on a church marquee captured the importance of first impressions. "You never get a second chance to make a good first impression."

Leaders should work at making a good first impression. This includes demeanor and dress. It is called impression management. Bill Horton Ph.D concluded, "First impressions are lasting impressions, and lasting impressions are usually manufactured."

People Are Good

"Variety is the spice of life." There are good traits in everyone and everyone is uniquely different. If every person you met were exactly like you, life would be monotonous, if not an endurance test. To say the least, it is a scary thought! Due diligence by an astute leader will reveal the exclusivity of an individual's life experience, talent, history, and culture. All offer untapped resources for creative management. Exploring "people resourcefulness" is an exciting, profitable adventure.

Watch for "Sleepers"

Degrees and credentialing are a fact of life in most career fields, but thinking "out of the box" may expand your horizons. When possible, it may be the right mix would include creative surprises with neither qualification. If your work force is sizeable, you have a catch of un-credentialed, teachable "sleepers" that could transform your organization. All they need is a leader to awaken them to the mission of the organization and a personal challenge to grow professionally. It is possible these individuals will be more readily responsive to the mission of your organization than those that are transplants from other organizations. A credentialed staff is essential in any selection process, but expertise, commitment, and qualifications cannot be overlooked.

Experienced leaders, in their quest for success, often overlook individuals that have the potential to be worth their weight in gold to the organization. These individuals do not hang out a shingle of self-importance. They know their abilities, perform well, and will move on to greener pastures when overlooked. (The leader that is preoccupied with his or her own personal ambitions frequently overlooks these "diamonds in the rough.") It would be interesting, and probably frightening, to know how costly this oversight has been to the average organization.

Learn from all you meet…learn diligently from the best in everyone you meet. Focus on strengths and learn from the strengths exhibited by others. Allow each person's uniqueness to be your tutor. If leaders would approach every individual as if that individual had the ability to perform some task better than anyone else, it would open new doors for creative growth within their organizations.

"Every man knows something that I do not know. I must probe until I find it; hence, all men are my teachers."
—Dr. Gustave Norling

If All the Trees Were Oaks

What if all the trees were oaks,
How plain the world would seem;
No maple syrup, banana splits,
And how would orange juice be?

Wouldn't it be a boring place,
If all the people were the same;
Just one color, just one language,
Just one family name!
-BUT-
If the forest were the world,
And all the people were the trees;
Palm and pine, bamboo and willow,
Live and grow in harmony.

Aren't you glad, my good friend,
Different though we be;
We are here to help each other,
I learn from you, and you, from me.
—Author Unknown

People Are Bad

"There is something good in everyone...but there is bad in all of us." People do things and say things they shouldn't do or say. All are susceptible; no one is perfect. The successful leader acknowledges this fact and prepares to creatively react to its inevitability. Naivety will result in vincibility to harmful consequences. Some people habitually indulge in destructive practices and perpetually involve themselves in adversarial behaviors. Some are jealous, others are responding to adverse life circumstances, or to individuals with whom they may differ. Some brag, some are dishonest, and others are deceitful. Some gossip, some circulate rumors, exaggerate, and lie. Successful leadership requires preparation for any and all of these eventualities.

"There's so much good in the worst of us, and so much bad in the best of us, that it behooves some of us not to talk about the rest of us."

"A stitch in time saves nine." One broken stitch, left unattended, will require more extensive tailoring at a later time. A single broken stitch can cause the garment to unravel. Immediate attention to a difficulty is often considered to be a nuisance, but experience will testify that prompt attention will prove to be less burdensome than time-consuming resolutions at a later date. Ignored small problems grow rapidly.

Timely conflict resolutions are imperative because problematic behaviors extend beyond the inevitable.

"Sow an act, and you reap a habit,
Sow a habit and you reap a character,
sow a character and you
Reap a destiny."
—Charles Reade

Timeliness is predicated on an acute sensitivity to subtle, but evident warning signs. I am delighted automobiles have evolved and we again have measurable gauges on the dashboard. There was a period of time when vehicles had only warning lights to signal malfunctions, or a need for service. Once the warning light appeared it was already too late. The damage was done. At least, with gauges, you can monitor the need for preventive maintenance. I may not be the "Tool Man," but I can read the gauges and know when there's a need to service the automobile. Sensitivity to warning signs is a skill that allows the leader to take preventive action, and be proactive in the implementation of conflict resolution measures.

The warning signs of bad behaviors are like billboards of the soul. They are demonstrations of a personal struggle and, at times, a call for help. Never trivialize another's problem. Problems are an exclusive obsession of the owner and, to the owner, deserving of a priority status. An acute sensitivity to subtle, but evident warning signs is crucial. Overt behaviors are used to disguise hurt, anger, fear, and jealousy. Self-imposed guilt can motivate the guilty to publicly focus on the same shortcomings in the lives of others. Unresolved conflicts with friends, spouses, and other acquaintances can be the culprit responsible for behavioral demonstrations. Financial adversities, stress, home pressures, and domestic conflict can, and do, contribute. Life circumstances can cause differing individuals to be jealous, negative, and critical.

Observant leaders learn without inquiry. The empathetic leader enhances his or her opportunity to constructively assist in a growth process. Learn to observe, learn to be sensitive, and learn to listen with your heart.

"Problems are only opportunities in work clothes."
—Henry J. Kaiser, American Industrialist

Ignoring a problem will only extend its life and scope. People problems always involve others. The intensity of a problem gains momentum when a leader chooses to "bury his head in the sand." The options are clear. You can acknowledge it or deny it. You can plan for it or act on impulse. You can learn from it or be overwhelmed by it. You can be an agent of change or be victimized by it. The choice is yours!

"You can't escape the responsibility of
tomorrow by evading it today."
—Abraham Lincoln

"If you're the boss and
your people fight you openly
when they think your wrong, that's healthy.

If your people fight each other openly in your presence
for what they believe in,
that's healthy.

But keep all communication
eyeball to eyeball."
—Robert Townsend

CHAPTER 3

PEOPLE BEHAVIORS

Use the leadership role to study hurtful behaviors. Insight will facilitate creativity.

People Talk

"A lie will travel around the world while truth gets its boots on!" Rumors and innuendos are hurtful and damaging. People love to talk. People who talk love to embellish their talk. We are storytellers, and the story must be interesting. Read your newspaper or watch your evening news; bad news is marketable. People love the sensational!

The tragic ending to fabricated stories is frightful. Those who hear the stories usually never hear, and most do not care to hear, the "rest of the story." The inability to recall the debilitating impact of reported error is a travesty of justice. There will always be those who hear the inaccuracy without the benefit of a correction. Prompt attention should be given to an urgent course of corrective action in order to address destructive talk.

"Birds of a feather flock together." People who love to gossip love people who love to gossip. They diligently seek out willing participants. Their circle of influence is predicated on their ability to report the unreportable and know the unknowable. This futile exercise destroys lives. Collaboration with others validates their own perceptions of reality, and co-dependent relationships, based on gossip, often emerge. Its destructive impact is so pronounced, it should be labeled, "a crime against humanity." It has the potential to destroy the spirit of an individual, making it an intrusion into the divine. It is a violation of another's dignity and reputation.

Gossip requires a participating listener. The listener is an integral component of the gossip process. Both are partners in the crime.

Without a listener, gossip dies a natural death. There is a term in Hebrew for gossip. It is called "Loshon Hora" (Loshon = tongue, Hora = evil). Loshon Hora, or gossip, is the same whether speaking it or listening to it. Even when what is said about a person is true, it is still Loshon Hora.

> "Gossip is when you hear something you like about someone you don't."
> —Earl Wilson, American newspaper columnist

The motivations may differ, but the result is always the same. Individuals are hurt, relationships are destroyed, and the strength of community is disabled. It may be a lack of inner peace, self-esteem, or accomplishment that brings inward feelings of inadequacy, resentment, and jealousy to the surface. Gossip can be used as an attempt to rationalize self-perceived inadequacies. One's failures can find expression in personal misery and unhappiness. It is true that, "Misery loves company."

Another dynamic exists in small communities. In close, or closed, social circles, gossip thrives as a favorite pastime and is considered harmless or even an enjoyable activity. So the full gamut of motivations could extend from "fun," to anger, to jealousy, to vindictiveness, or maliciousness. Ironically, participants who become victims feel differently when the talk focuses on them.

> "Great minds discuss ideas, average minds discuss events, and small minds discuss people."
> —Hyman G. Rickover, Admiral, U.S. Navy

Gossip should never be tolerated. Malicious gossip requires urgency. Malicious gossip always intensifies and, if not addressed, will lead to character assassination. Leaders live in "glass houses," and many that follow enjoy breaking windows. Leaders become prime targets for gossip due to their decision-making roles and their extensive exposure. The more visible a person is, the more susceptible they are to gossip. No leadership job description ever required one to become a doormat.

The consistent practice of truth principles is your credentialing to confront your accusers. Confrontational truth will discredit gossip. The leader under siege must stay the course, exercise truth, and refuse to be distracted by misrepresentations of fact. Earned respect pays big dividends. Truth invested will produce credibility and respect. Truth is your greatest ally when individuals gossip. It is the only prevention and possible cure for gossip.

Heads Up!

Your response to reports is crucial to the resolution. Don't permit your demeanor and comments to betray you. Your actions may be opportunistically interpreted and you may not recognize the revised version of fact. A display of shock, dismay, angry denial, or even an attempt to bring a hasty resolution to gossip can be sordidly used against you. Think before you act, then act! Be careful with timelines. One can act too swiftly, but there can be danger in delay. I recall a recently observed bumper sticker that read, "Ever stop to think and forget to start again?"

Some become proficient in the solicitation of ill reports. They are very adept in effectively creating disenchantment through both third party and their own flagrant reports. The pleasure of reporting any solicited negative comment from the listener breathes new life into their contemptible value system. Any sympathetic response is an affirmation, and provides them the license to recite the statement to others as an endorsement of their own opinion. It proves their point. Others, too, are disenchanted. The anonymity of, "they said," pales in comparison to the unintended personalized testimonial. It is a potent tool in the work chest of the proverbial "troublemaker."

Rumor Control

Gossip is defined as rumors and conjectures (guesses) about others. Gossip has an ulterior motive, It is designed to degrade, belittle, or instigate negative consequences for others. It can be communicated verbally or non-verbally. Silence, a grimace, a wink, or a facial expression in response to a derogatory comment can speak more loudly than any verbalized message.

Gossip is based on speculations, assumptions, and misinformation. It is self-destructive for the perpetrator and destructive for the victim. It is emotionally detrimental to all individuals involved in its circulation, and it is financially costly to an organization.

Gossip is a character issue. The person that engages in gossip demonstrates they personally have a character deficiency that will negatively impact all with whom they come in contact. Their actions are indiscriminant. If they gossip to you about someone else, they will gossip to someone else about you.

"The measure of a man's real character is what he would do if he would never be found out."

—Thomas Macauley

Leadership Style Can Stimulate Talk

Leadership creates environment! Never be guilty of creating an environment that stimulates excessive talk. Leadership should be committed to a "rumor free" work environment. Precautionary action, if effective, must emerge from the leader's own commitment to credibility and truth. Secrecy, negligence, dishonesty, broken confidentiality, and failure to support delegated responsibilities fuel rumor mills. The long-term implications of talk emphasizes its liability potential. Talk will not go away, will not change, and will be exaggerated when not addressed.

It is possible the leader's personal conduct can be the mysterious leak and the identity of the unidentifiable, "they said," perpetrator. Poor planning, inconsistencies, poor communication, adverse consequences of unneeded changes, and failure to acknowledge mistakes are only a few of the reasons leaders generate their own rumor mills. Leaders must be careful when "thinking out loud." With whom, and under what circumstances planning efforts are shared, can stimulate speculations that are subsequently verbalized. Discretion is advised to determine who will use or misuse information. Contemplations can quickly be circulated as fact. Leaders inadvertently spawn gossip when they share delicate information. Careless conversations or innuendoes related to personal career goals can be misconstrued. Poor communication or speculations regarding leadership planning can be interpreted as directives by even those committed to your goals. Certainly those that are not supportive of your objectives, if vindictive, will seize opportunities to become "spin doctors."

Some leaders have been known to cleverly spawn opportunistic rumors for effect. These antics are always self-serving and apparent to all except the perpetrator. Generally, the harshness of the consequences are fitting for the crime.

Precautionary measures to prevent rumors are thwarted when the leader is careless in the selection of his consultation resources, or ignores counsel for selfish, ambitious reasons. Leaders have been known to "go through the motions" of seeking counsel when already knowing their course of action.

> "Many receive advice, few profit by it."
>   —Publilius Syrus (1st century B.C.)

Leadership is a lonely role. The leader is submerged in people and activity, but is burdened with un-delegable, decision-making responsibilities. "The buck stops here" is a lonely responsibility, and advisors are "a dime a dozen."

In summary, it is inexcusable for a person in a leadership role to participate in rumors. Critical comments, whether careless or premeditated, are inexcusable. To maliciously critique or criticize subordinates or peers with other peers is self-destructive. Such a practice undermines credibility and ensures ineffectiveness.

> James 3:8
> "But the tongue can no man tame; it is an unruly evil, full of deadly poison."
>   —King James Version

Your At Risk

Don't let your guard down! You too, without realizing it, can become a participant in GOSSIP. Your risk is greater because your exposure is greater. The frequency of your exposure and the volume of information available to you in your leadership role will emphasize your need for caution. This is the reason it is imperative that any exposure should trigger an immediate, constructive response to destructive talk. This is responsible leadership. Be alert to the fact, stressful leadership responsibilities, destructive talk, and unresolved conflicts contribute to your vulnerability.

Don't "stew" over excessive talk; address it. Carrying the baggage of anxiety for too long a period will impair your judgment. Dr. Harry Stack Sullivan understood anxiety to be that which one experiences when one's self-esteem is threatened. Avoid a "thin-skinned" response to criticism. The temptation may cause you to share your grievances with those who have no need to know. This, too, is gossip!

Sour Grape Mentality

"A rotten apple will spoil the entire barrel." Remember, some relationships, work or otherwise, are sustained on a "sour grape" mentality. Verbalized negativism will energize the private misunderstandings or misconceptions embraced by others. It exaggerates dormant frustrations, gripes, and negativity.

Embellishment is the spice that seasons negativity. Personalized differences emotionalize the misbehavior. Like gossipers, negative people find one another on the radar screen of life. They, too, are good at building co-dependent relationships.

Negative talk is contagious and always counterproductive. Any exposure enhances your chances of participation. Even casual exposure generates unproductive potentialities. It will always create an unpleasant work environment. It makes others uncomfortable, can be embarassing, and might even result in a perceived need to reveal derogatory information. The motivational factors between negative attitudes and gossip are of similar origins.

Confidentiality

People talk, and they will. Reports, with "confidentiality" stamped all over them have been creatively recycled. Some hearers are provided their greatest temptation when a report is prefaced by, "You're the only one I've told," "Don't tell a soul," or some other tantalizing comment. It provides the same inspiration as a "Wet Paint" sign.

Confidential information is a sacred trust. It is sacred because you possess another's private information. Confidential information preserves another's right to privacy. It engages the emotions of who one is, what they are all about, and the perceptions others will have, if private information is made public. The threat of hurt is not superficial. The possibility of disclosure stimulates anxiety, fear, and anger. To break confidentiality violates and victimizes the vulnerable. Even casual exposure to confidential information makes you personally accountable for that information. The recipients of such information are placed in a steward's role. Stewardship requires confidential responsibility.

Circulation of any report carries with it consequences. Others should not be burdened with the responsibility of information for which they have no constructive use. The unauthorized transferal of confidential information terminates life long relationships. Broken confidentiality is a betrayal.

Forgiveness may be obtained, but the loss of trust is terminal. Be cautiously discreet with whom you share confidential information.

Broken confidences, even if intended for good, will come back to haunt you. Neither the need for consultation, nor exasperating circumstances are justifications for a leader to share confidential information. Well-intended efforts to assist can go awry when confidential information is exchanged. "The chickens will always come home to roost," and the consequences are irreparable.

Expect Criticism

Expect criticism! Vocal criticisms are activated by disparate motivations. Many have already been identified. Public officials and leaders, in the spotlight of life, are subjected to a cycle of exultation, efflorescence, and effacement. The same individuals that praise you will later condemn you. You can do everything right and still receive criticism. You're in good company. Christ lived a perfect life and they crucified Him.

His life commitment was to all, critics included. His redemptive purposes were often linked to humanitarian need. He fed the hungry and cared for the sick. He confirmed that the spiritual and physical are intricately woven together. His best efforts for others did not make him immune to criticism. You should not expect more. Life is a succession of acquaintances and relationships that expose us to the criticism of others. Relationships and criticism are easy to come by, but friends freed of this vice are a real find.

Five days before His crucifixion He was given the "red carpet treatment" by the residents of Jerusalem. They rolled out the red carpet, took their coats from their backs, and laid them on the ground. On the back of a donkey, traveling on a garment-paved roadway, they honored His entrance into the city. They waved palm branches and proclaimed Him, "King!" I have often wondered of their whereabouts five days later when in public ridicule, the throngs screamed, "Crucify Him!" The truth is, in the period of one week, from lips of blessing proceeded cursing. It is another vivid reminder of the power and influence of criticism. Caustic words are germinal. Even His closest friends distanced themselves from Him, and one, whom he privately coached, publicly used profanity to deny he ever knew Him. The leader who doesn't expect criticism or cannot handle it is not leadership material. "If you can't stand the heat, get out of the kitchen."

Valid or invalid criticisms should always get our attention. Don't over-react and, "throw caution to the wind." If valid, and often they are, value the criticism and constructively act upon it. If invalid, reckless zeal may lend it credibility. Certainly an obsession to over-react to every negative comment will only extend the life of criticism and give it the appearance of credibility. Criticisms that are known to be vindictive best accomplish their purpose when the leader overreacts or retaliates. Be cautious, an improper reaction will only serve those who criticize you.

Important Reminders:

1. Usually your critics are small in number, and the attention you give the criticism will either curtail the criticism or broadcast it.
2. If the criticisms are numerous, or wide spread, they could indicate a leadership flaw.
3. When addressing vindictive criticism, don't shoot all the ducks in the pond to bag your critic.
4. A public rebuke to stop criticism will extend the life and outreach of criticisms. Use caution when publicly addressing your critics. You can do more harm than good.
5. Inspiration, not repudiation, will challenge your productive staff and diminish the influence of your critics.
6. Face to face encounters reduce the shelf life of spurious criticisms.

The inevitability of criticisms should never cause one to acquiesce, or succumb to a self-fulfilling prophecy. Criticism is based on perceptions. These may be right, or wrong. Perceptions, to the individual, are real, and influence the actions of an individual. Verbalized criticisms reflect a person's struggle with life. There is truth, to a greater or lesser degree, reflected in perceptions, and sometimes truth is extremely painful. All have a constant need for growth and improvement. Agreement or disagreement is not the issue; self-assessment to determine the validity of a perception is all-important.

Accept criticism! Allow it to tutor you. If it has validity, you can benefit from the learning experience. Don't fear it, embrace it! "Take the lemons and make lemonade." If it has no validity, it should prompt a careful reassessment of your actions. A misunderstood or poorly communicated explanation for your actions can lead to misperceptions. This is not to imply an explanation is needed for every action taken, but if it impacts the lives of individuals, or your organization, an explanation is crucial. If the criticism is a malicious misrepresentation, and you feel as if you are unjustly being "shot at," a prompt, truthful response can quickly remove the ammunition from your critic's gun.

Two temptations should be avoided at all cost. The first is the delusion that you can coddle or charm your critic into an agreeable alliance. Coddling and charm will more often than not drive your criticism underground. It then operates under the radar screen. At the very least, it only extends the life of the injustice and delays the inevitable. The second is the attempt to counteract criticism with self-praise or overwhelming reports of your successes. Self-reported adulations only load your critic's gun and lend credibility to the criticism.

The reader may challenge the following statement, especially if he or she is presently enduring unjust criticism. Experience has proven criticism is needed. The cycle of exultation and efflorescence can spin out of control without a reality check. An occasional dose of criticism and a taste of "humble pie" can actualize reality. Every leader needs it and must learn to live with it. Develop a rapport that welcomes constructive criticism. It will prevent destructive criticism. Everyone needs a system of checks and balances. When criticized, assess before you act. If the criticism is true, untrue, or partially true, seize the moment as a growth opportunity. If flippant nonsense, move on!

"If you wish to drown, do not torture yourself with shallow water."
—Bulgarian proverb

People Make Mistakes

Chronic Patterns

"Some people never learn." People make mistakes. There are those that seem destined to repeat their mistakes. Evidence of this pattern can be observed in the lives of those who experience a succession of hurtful and harmful relationships. Self-fulfilled prophecies of failure are perpetuated in their life experience. The ability to constructively redirect a life circumstance seems to be an insurmountable feat to some, while to others it is little more than mental conditioning.

"Lord deliver me from the man who never makes a mistake, and also from the man who makes the same mistake twice."
—Dr. William J. Mayo, founder, Mayo Clinic

Potential for Growth

We all experience physical growth and we all learn. Growth patterns may be accelerated, abnormal, or delayed, but birth does initiate growth. Anything that is born experiences growth! With growth comes learning. The ability to learn is predicated on the strengths of an individual. Some are endowed with multiple strengths while others appear to be extremely limited. Make it your personal challenge to change lives by seizing every opportunity to develop minuscule strengths. Some experience a delay in the learning process due to a disability, others by a deliberate choice.

Structure for Growth

"You can't educate what you can't control." Educators research innovative educational approaches and select the best available curriculum to stimulate learning. Learning is always impacted by life experiences. It is either enhanced or delayed. "Live and learn" is an accepted, but questionable, truism. Life is a learning experience, but learning requires more than living, it requires discipline. Educators have long recognized the fact that discipline, personal or otherwise, is critical to the learning process. Creativity to provide structure for growth requires a time commitment from leadership.

Experience for Growth

"If you ignore the mistakes of the past, you are destined to repeat them in the future." We know people can, do, and will make mistakes. "Do people learn from their mistakes?" has been a long debated question. Some people learn from their mistakes, and those who do, learn more quickly because of those mistakes. Every mistake is a growth opportunity for all that are affected by the mistake. The one having committed the mistake can, experientially, glean preventive insights, and those affected can learn to create proactive resolutions.

Hot Horseshoe!

One version of a circulated story illustrates the point. Upon entering the frontier community, the senses of a stranger are drawn to the pungent smell of smoke and the methodic ring of a hammer stroke on an anvil. Intrigued, the "greenhorn" followed his senses to the shop of the local blacksmith. His unannounced arrival and the nature of the blacksmith's work dictated the course of events.

The blacksmith's forehead glistened with perspiration as he quickly removed a searing red-hot horseshoe from the open furnace door. With tongs in hand, he gingerly placed the horseshoe on the anvil. The greenhorn's unobserved entry, accompanied by a guttural clearing of his throat startled the blacksmith as he turned to toss the tongs to one side. The distraction of the greenhorn and the pursuing pleasantries allowed the shoe to blacken quickly.

The greenhorn's awkwardness to make conversation was noticeable, but his subsequent action was not. Without inquiry, the visitor unwittingly reached for the blackened horseshoe. The subtle action was so swift and surprising, there wasn't time to sound an alarm. The greenhorn's intention to make conversation with horseshoe in hand was brutally interrupted by writhing pain. Frantically, he hurled the shoe to the floor. As the flooring smoldered around the horseshoe, the bemused blacksmith inquired, "Son, was it hot?" After regaining his composure, the hurting, embarrassed stranger replied, "No, sir! It just doesn't take long to look at a horseshoe." The pain of a mistake can accelerate the learning process.

"Freedom is not worth having if it does not include the freedom to make mistakes."

—Mahatma Gandhi

Leadership Mistakes

"Fix it and forget it." Leadership requires resiliency. Contrary to the biased utopian world of news media experts, individuals who lead will make mistakes. Leaders who perform make mistakes. Those who do not perform make neither mistakes nor progress. Only armchair quarterbacks and news media experts imply perfection.

The profundity of news commentators eliminates the need for the general public to think for themselves. The exclusivity of their intellectualism equates the actions and opinions of politicians, ministers, educators, scientists, literary giants, scholars, and peons to the elementary classroom. Excuse my levity, but the rationale of the absurdities of their daily critique provides fodder for fun.

Intelligentsia is not confined to the newsroom, so "fess up" and move on! Attempts to cover up, "pass the buck," or rationalize are counterproductive and only serve to extend the life of the mistake. Your leadership role can be jeopardized and may even be contingent on the wisdom you display in addressing your mistakes. The frequency of published accounts of cover-ups by politicians, medical practitioners, educators, clergy, and yes, even the news media are only a few of the vivid reminders of this truth. The lessons gleaned from the outcome of any and all of these reports should significantly heighten your sensitivity.

Timeliness is everything. Act immediately! Candid disclosure and corrective action are important to the individuals that have been harmed by a mistake. Ignored mistakes can be egregious. Corrective action is a process that requires time, predicated on the intensity of the consequences. The duration and extent of influence usually determine intensity. It is always advisable to remember the adage, "the sooner, the better."

The fallacy of belaboring the mistake is the flip side of the coin. While some forget the lessons of the past, others remorsefully remember the pain. Both are equally devastating dynamics. To allow vision, ambition, and drive to be permanently impaired by a preoccupation with the mistakes of the past will make the leader a casualty of the mistake. Self-pity, penance, or fear, can immobilize a leader. The option is yours. Rehabilitate your emotions, or lean on the crutch of inactivity.

"Don't grieve over spilled milk." Don't allow a mistake to be emotionally debilitating. Internalizing "what ifs" will result in a consequential "what will be." Hindsight is luxury. Hindsight is 20/20 vision! The accuracy and elusiveness of hindsight are certainties that are only accessible after the fact. We can learn invaluable lessons from hindsight, but cannot alter or retrieve the act from which the lesson originated.

Life does go on, and lessons learned can prevent a repeat of yesterday's mistakes. We are destined to repeat unlearned lessons from history. Learn all you can as quickly as you can. The person who never makes a mistake doesn't exist. The person who deceivingly says they have never made a mistake is the person who admits they have never done anything worth doing.

"If we could be twice young and twice old we could correct all our mistakes."

—Euripides (ca.484-406 B.C.) Greek Dramatist

Mistakes will affect the bottom line. They are emotionally and financially costly.

Leadership Competency

"A leader is a dealer in hope."

—Napoleon Bonaparte

Mistakes reveal a leader's astuteness. They provide leaders an opportunity to assess their own leadership style and competencies, as well as their ability to identify opportunistic challenges for developmental growth in the lives of those they lead.

Caution!

Competency is two-dimensional when dealing with the mistakes made by subordinates. Not only must the leader be competent to recognize growth potential, the leader must act decisively. Leadership incompetence could be the contributing factor if chronic patterns persist.

Competency Checks

Mistakes by subordinates may be a measure of the leader's competency, not an indicator of staff incompetence. Overworked staff or insensitivity to unrealistic work assignments create errors. An apparent lack of direction, or displays of anger confuse those under your leadership. Any subterfuge to smoke screen a lack of direction will cause resentment. To use an earlier analogy, when your proven performers begin to make mistakes, you may need to check the gauges on the dashboard. You may be out of gas or over heating. The degree of leadership incompetence is best measured by the frequency of your bad judgment.

Competency on the part of a leader requires:

1. Recognition of the learning opportunity
2. Creativity to capitalize on the opportunity
   a. Sensitivity to one's vulnerability
   b. Awareness of the need for direction
3. Initiative to act in a timely manner to seize the moment
   a. For desired change
   b. For required discipline

Demeanor

The competent leader must not communicate, consciously, or subconsciously, demeaning ridicule or condemnation. The offender is usually the first to recognize their mistake, and knows best the temperature of the horseshoe. It is the leader's responsibility to know best the energizing possibilities of the growth potential. The leader's capacity to accept the inevitability of mistakes will determine the leader's effectiveness to facilitate growth. Attentiveness to timely intervention enhances the learning curve stimulated by the mistake.

The Power of Denial

Delay and denial are symptoms of incompetence. Ignoring or denying reality and failing to listen when being advised of problematic areas can make others susceptible to mistakes. The failure to resolve issues and communicate effectively will create a fertile environment that recycles mistakes.

Denial is a disbelief of and contradiction of reality. It prohibits rehabilitation for addictive behaviors. One aspect of drug addiction is the inability to deal with the obvious. The similarity is frightening. Denial redefines reality. It allows a person to pursue their perceptions and point of view without concern for their own well being or the well being of others. Disfigured reality will result in consequential abnormalities. In fact, denial of a problem only exaggerates the problem.

A leader prone to the denial of reality should be sensitive to these implications. The exercise of denial can become habitual. The revision of reality not only becomes a habit, it becomes an end within itself. A person who rehearses a revision of reality soon believes his or her own lie. The behavior leads to deceitfulness, dishonesty, and an overestimation of one's discernment. It is the opposite spectrum of common sense thinking. It is irrational thinking.

People Have To Be Corrected

Empathize!

When I accepted my first significant leadership role, a senior colleague, with forty plus years of experience, gave me the best advice I ever received. He said, "In your role, there will be times when you have to rebuke people because of their conduct." He advised, "Don't ever rebuke anyone until you can laugh or cry about it." The ability to empathize, feel the hurt, and emotionally relate to the misconduct will dramatically impact unpleasant encounters. Synergetic energy stimulates growth.

Control Your Emotions

"Don't criticize the Indian that limps until you've worn his moccasins." Anger, resentment, personal vendettas, or ulterior motives inhibit empathy or sympathy. The ability to feel the pain and understand the reason is a prerequisite to rebuke. Destructive consequences can be unleashed by either the unmerited or the unprofessional authoritarian rebuke. The rippling effect of such action perpetuates an infectious ill will.

Investigate

Investigate before you choose your penalty. If you're too busy to investigate you're too busy to lead. A person must be perceived as innocent until proven guilty. Once guilt is confirmed, appropriate disciplinary action can be exercised. Correction is an emotional experience for all parties involved in the process. It requires time and understanding.

The leader's motive must be pure. It will prove to be either destructive or constructive. Destructive corrective measures are those that are initiated in the wrong way, at the wrong place, and at the wrong time. Constructive correction, again, is a competency measurement. Your approach, timing, and motive are all critical to the process. You personally control the process and bear the responsibility for the outcome.

"Step up to the plate," "Take the bull by the horns" and assume your responsibility. "Lead, follow, or get out of the way!" Cowardice or respectful boldness, caring candidness or timidity, the choices are yours. Corrective action is never pleasant but it is a requirement of leadership. Taking the "easy way out" is a guarantee the problem requiring the action will not be resolved and the action will have adverse consequences. Aversive action is not evasive action. It is neither deceptive nor delayed. Face the problem and do it quickly. Confrontation does not necessarily equate to an altercation. If the encounter is handled properly and it does result in an altercation, it is proof positive the action was merited.

Being Liked

Often leaders are remiss with corrective action because they want to be liked. It is admirable, but it is not an entitlement for the leader. It is a dividend. Be careful with inconsistent leniency to engender the favors of others. The motive for the desire is crucial. Motivations designed to enhance one's ego cannot be concealed. Character driven genuineness is imperative when discipline is required. Genuineness cannot be cloned. Character traits speak more loudly than verbalized proclamations.

Big egos can be a stumbling block to appropriate corrective measures. If you do struggle with an ego problem, that should be your first priority. Big egos distort reality. Big egos demand attention; the wrong kind of attention. Ego driven attention will not permit you to ingratiate yourself to others. Old timers assessed big egos with a simple analogy. "Some people are too big for their britches." If you become a legend in your own mind, you will be the worst of nightmares to those you lead. The covert shrewdness of an inflated ego is manifested in self-deception. The person wearing the big britches is the last to recognize they're too large. Early detection by others will make any overture on your part opportunistic. Egotism is immune to reality.

As a leader, you need to be knowledgeable, respected, and trustworthy. Everyone will not like you. If everyone appears to, don't believe it. If everyone does, your leadership may be stagnant. The desire to be liked can become an obsessive, all consuming leadership style that quickly becomes the object of scorn. Your behavior will be erratic and your decisions inconsistent. The individual that makes the most noise will gain the greatest favor, and they become repeat customers. Every decision you make will be skewed. You will second-guess and take action to override the good judgment of supervisors under your leadership for a pitiful pittance of praise. You will pay a big price for a product you will never receive. You will engage in shadow boxing. The elusive figure will eventually score the knock-out punch.

Deal with the Perpetrator

An attempt to avoid personalized corrective action by generalizing punitive measures is a transparent practice. This is self-deception. Your ploy to avoid personal confrontation will only elicit the disfavor of all. Surreptitious action is worse than no action at all. If a subordinate does not perform or becomes a troublemaker, a one-on-one encounter is required. Anything less will not suffice. Memos written to the general work population to address the infraction of one employee makes a private matter a public issue. Penalizing everyone for the misbehaviors of a few invites controversy. You don't pull all the plants out of the garden to remove the weeds. You remove the weeds and nurture the plants. Your inaction will be perceived as weakness.

Use of the garden analogy could impart additional insight. The seeds of deception are the weeds that will devour your garden. Weeds grow profusely in poor soil, require little moisture, and their removal very laborious.

Self-esteem Fallacies

Another frequented rationalization is the fear that punitive actions are harmful to the self-esteem of those corrected. This is not true when the action is properly administered. More will be said later on the subject of punitive action.

It is important that today's leader remember that many you lead may have had little exposure to absolutes and corrective measures. Their developmental years may bear the imprint of self-esteem modalities. Pardon my digression, but I feel a comment is required. The pendulum has swung. It is now embraced by many in child development that children need a balance of praise and dispraise. It is as important for children to be confronted with their failures as it is to have their successes rewarded and reinforced.

As in the formative years, individuals need approval for motivation, and disapproval to deter unacceptable behavior. Past emphasis on self-esteem gave self-esteem a life of its own that proved to be counterproductive, unrealistic, and detrimental to healthy behavioral patterns. The very fact that this acknowledgment is included in a book on common sense probably brings a chuckle from the grave of our forebears.

Handle With Extreme Care

Corrective action is not a license for abusive action. Misuse or abuse of an individual is never acceptable. Autocratic leadership that opportunistically brutalizes an individual can result in irreparable emotional damage. The vulnerability of the corrective experience is a sacred trust. Too, the moment should never be seized to vent resentment and anger due to the leader's own pent-up hostility over a failure to routinely address adverse behaviors.

Making a staff member cry is no mark of greatness and certainly not a commendable leadership trait. To aggrandize such juvenile behavior as staff development adds insult to injury. The act decries the logic of leadership. This behavior speaks more to the leader's struggle with his or her role and the imprint adverse circumstances in life have had on their own psyche.

Corrective Action By Proxy

Proxy is giving authority for one to act for another. Some choose to take corrective action by proxy. Using opportunistic, inappropriate, measures to cloak intent and circumvent an ethical, direct, constructive approach to communicate corrective action. Communication is impersonal and conveyed by a third party. Secondhand messages become the first line of defense. Secondhand messages are fragile. They are disrespectful, will be misunderstood, and will be resented by all recipients.

Corrective directives are communicated through memos, e-mail messages, revised policies and procedures, and a succession of written warnings. Corrective action by proxy often assigns personnel action responsibilities to subordinates. Correction by proxy dehumanizes, demoralizes, and discourages your staff. It masks the leader's fears and inability to lead. Only leaders who are uncertain of their skills attempt corrective action by proxy. This secondhand process uses others and other things as a means to an end.

Personal Relationships

Corrective action for a personal friend or acquaintance is problematic. Relationships make difficult issues more complex. All meaningful resolutions require you to separate the person from the problem! A laser focus upon the problem, the consequences, and the resolution is primary. The resolution must be impartial and not be influenced by the relationship. True friendships can and do short-circuit the process. The essence of friendship encumbers equity. This negative impact on the resolution process is only the precursor to subsequent difficulties. Relationships impede prudent corrective measures. The practice of recuse in a court of law acknowledges the fragility of prudence when subjected to relationships.

Value Time and Humor

Adequate time is needed to allow a "cooling off" period. Proper timing will facilitate understanding, and convenience the appropriate use of humor. It has been my experience that humor, in certain situations, is more effective as corrective action and can even be used in difficult circumstances as a reprimand. If humor can be interjected after the fact, and after all parties have had time to assess the behavior, it can have a surprising impact. Upon reflection, the foolishness of misbehavior is often humorous. Engaging an individual in laughter over the absurdity of an unpleasant situation may be the best medicine. It is less threatening, and it always tastes better. It is true, "More can be said with a smile, than could ever be said with a frown."

Avoid Punitive Reactions

Corrective measures are generally considered to be punitive. When this is true, the result is always the same. Hard feelings, anger, resentment, and retaliation take precedence over the corrective action. The focus of attention is on the person, not the problem. Positive resolutions are not compatible with punitive objectives. Punitive action is a reflection of leadership style. It is, at times, the expression of stress and professional burnout. At other times, it is an outburst of pent up emotions over self-inflicted leadership deficiencies. "You can catch more flies with honey than you can with vinegar."

Only an insecure leader will publicly rebuke subordinates. It validates ineptness and is a subterfuge. If done in the presence of uninvolved parties, it makes the act more egregious. The embarrassment experienced by the subordinate is only surpassed by the embarrassment of the observer. The conduct, even if the allegation should be true, invalidates a leader, and it always confirms a lack of leadership experience.

"You do not lead by hitting people over the head – that's assault, not leadership."

—Dwight Eisenhower

Learn the Importance of Timeliness

The failure to timely address staff deficiencies, or act on misbehaviors emotionally internalizes and personalizes the behaviors of others. When problems are internalized, the leader must prepare for an emotional roller coaster ride that can lead to poor health and psychosomatic symptoms. "It may not be what you're eating that causes your bad health, it may be what's eating on you." Ignored problems, and a " bury your head in the sand" routine, will escalate problems to full fruition and unbearable consequences.

One Size Doesn't Fit All!

There is no "cookie cutter" solution to the multiple variables that produce misunderstandings and improper behaviors. Every problem is unique and every problem, if resolved, requires a personal touch. When problematic areas, or individuals, are identifiable and persistent patterns of behavior reflect destructive trends, personalized attention is required. The integrity of the leader is at stake. Simple courtesy and honesty demands both a constructive encounter and appropriate disclosure of destructive behaviors with the identified perpetrator.

The leader that resorts to any process that punishes everyone, or involves others in a decision that only the leader should make, will create ill-will, suspicions, and misperceptions by productive staff persons. Subtle, evasive, or perceived ingenious processes that circumvent the simple courtesy of a face-to-face confrontation, will needlessly publicize what should be a private matter.

The implications of a leader using others to facilitate difficult decisions will not only make an unpleasant experience worse, it will give birth to resentful and unproductive relationships. Problems, private or public, are best resolved private and personally. The dignity of all parties involved can best be preserved with a little "common sense." The leader who succumbs to fear and compromises on misbehaviors will inspire reprehensible conduct patterns.

It is important to more carefully examine the time, place, and way corrective measures are conducted.

THE PROPER TIME should be predicated on the following:

AFTER...
1. Anger has subsided.
2. A thorough examination of the facts.
3. The person has had the opportunity to provide an explanation.

AND BEFORE...
1. You allow resentment to affect your judgment.

2. The conduct has an adverse affect on others.
3. It becomes detrimental to the perpetrator.

THE PROPER PLACE should be:

PRIVATE...
1. Where conversation cannot be overheard.
2. Where others cannot speculate on the intent of the meeting.

NOT PUBLIC...
1. Competent leaders do not rebuke publicly. This practice publicizes a leader's ineptness.
2. Don't be a coward and use your position, or a public setting under your control, to impart a rebuke you fail to have the courage to address one-on-one.
3. Public intimidation will always spawn private retaliation.

COMFORTABLE...
1. Where both parties can be comfortable.
2. Where the perpetrator will not be made to feel subservient.

CONDUCIVE TO POSITIVE OUTCOMES...

THE PROPER WAY should be:

1. One-on-one.
2. Confidential.
3. With sincere concern.
4. Free of anger.
5. Constructive.
6. Honest.
7. Candid.
8. Frank.
9. Non-intimidating.

REMEMBER... the RESPECT you demonstrate will be the return you realize on your investment!

People Solve Problems

Conflict Resolution

Much has been written and excellent resources are available to provide strategies for conflict resolution. Leaders should be diligent in the development of effective conflict resolution skills. The multiplicity of "people dynamics" creates an array of challenging scenarios. Required brevity, when addressing these complexities, makes any comment on the subject appear simplistic.

Ownership

A safe premise is ownership. No person can, or will, solve a problem until he or she claims ownership. Leadership must strive to facilitate this growth goal. A constructive, confrontational approach with the source of the report and the responsible party is always imperative to shorten the life of error. When quarreling parties are involved, all participants in the incident must be given the opportunity to orderly discuss allegations or differences in a face-to-face arrangement. I have observed that people who are prone to talk negatively of others are less talkative when face-to-face encounters are arranged.

Face-to-face encounters, with the subject of their discussions, give individuals a greater incentive to be committed to ownership and the resolution of a problem. A by-product of this resolution process is the preventive measures generated by the required accountability for one's actions. It will prove to be an effective deterrent in the future.

Truth Opportunities

The difference between the truth and a lie is, you have to remember a lie, but you don't the truth. A bumper sticker captures this thought: "Truth is easier to remember than a lie." Truth is a process of natural recall, while a lie is a self-serving fabrication, susceptible to memory inaccuracies. Meetings designed for conflict resolution and problem solving should be considered truth opportunities. Such meetings ensure that misrepresentations of the truth are difficult for the perpetrator. This is the reason contradictions are easily identified in constructive confrontational encounters. Leadership should be prepared to facilitate an equitable procedure that makes the experience as constructive as possible for all participating parties. These encounters should be thoroughly documented. Remember, a lie is defined as "an attempt to deceive without the other's consent."

Neutrality

A word of caution, do not become a participant, do not take sides, and be sure you permit the participants to solve the problem. Commitment to a consistent, constructive, confrontational, conflict resolution process will create an environment of expectancy. Accountability for criticisms, rumors, and idle talk is a powerful dynamic that works! It enhances productive work relationships and discourages destructive habits.

Consistency

Consistency in the implementation of these growth opportunities will curtail rumors, prevent their circulation, and force responsible parties to come out of concealment. An effective, consistent policy will accommodate the leader because it will:

1. Sort out the truth.
2. Stop destructive gossip.
3. Identify the source.
4. Immediately provide problem solving information.
5. Eliminate the "middle man."
6. Deprive the carrier of the bad news the pleasure derived from reporting it.
7. Force the perpetrator to claim ownership of the problem.
8. Act as a preventive measure.

When individuals accept the responsibility of ownership, they learn to be innovative in the prevention process.

"Handle with Care"

"You can't win them all." There will be times when efforts you make to create growth opportunities for problematic individuals are futile. In the corrective process, you should expect success, but prepare for failure. When mentoring, coaching, and corrective measures fail to produce results, action must be taken. Good documentation of these preventive measures will support a justifiable decision when dealing with a "no-win" situation.

It may become necessary that your failed attempts require you to confront the difficult behavior with constructive alternatives. The subject can be broached by your stated interest in their personal and professional growth. It should be acknowledged that their conduct suggests they are unhappy in their present employment role. You may then offer your assistance in helping them focus on a more challenging, or enjoyable employment environment.

Termination responsibilities conjure up ambivalent feelings. It is an emotional experience. Anxiety, empathy, anger, sympathy, trepidation, and even fear can all be experienced in any given termination process.

The perpetrator's misbehavior, too, is a culmination of an emotional experience that found its origin in a conditioned thought process that most likely included resentment, jealousy, greed, or lackadaisical practices. The poor behaviors by some may be chronic and have life long origins. Emotional feelings can impact sound judgment on the part of both parties involved in the confrontational process. Everything about the process should be stamped, "Handle with care."

It is important that the termination of an individual be:
1. Positive
2. Supportive
3. Empathetic
4. Based on documented evidence

The termination finalizes the action for the infractions. It is possible to energize the problem after the resolution with careless conversation.

> "Every
> problem
> contains
> within itself
> the seeds
> of its
> own
> Solution."
> —Bits and Pieces

"The wise
learn from experience.

The wisest
learn from the experience
of others."
—Unknown

"True
leadership
must be for the
benefit of the followers,
not the
enrichment
of the
leaders."
—Robert Townsend

CHAPTER 4

PEOPLE POWER

Build Your Own

Your success is contingent on "People Power." "People Power" resources are twofold. Leaders can be recruited from other organizations or developed internally from the existing work force. Outstanding performers, developed by previous employers, can offer fresh perspectives and contribute greatly, so long as their energy and expertise are compatible with your leadership philosophy and can be channeled into your organizational goals. Don't be surprised if these successful, high achievers are so preoccupied with their own personal career goals, that their potential is more detrimental than productive. Ambitious personal career goals can disrupt successful operations and retard organizational growth.

It is my opinion these resources should only be utilized when expertise or qualified resources are not internally available. This resource is the gold in your own back yard. It may take some effort to extract it from the earth, but it can be a rewarding find. Every organization has individuals "in waiting." They only need to be discovered, nurtured, mentored, and developed. These individuals have a greater inclination to be committed to your organizational goals. The leader who learns to build people will harness the full potential of "People Power."

> "Good management consists in showing people how to do the work of superior people."
>
> —John Rockefeller, Jr.

Helping a person discover his or her own inherent strength is the foundational stone upon which you must build. Discovery can be a lengthy process, and you must expect limitations in assisting individuals in this undertaking. The "baggage" of experiential failures or personality quirks presents unique and exciting challenges. These "diamonds in the rough" will produce great wealth, but the cutting and polishing may be a tedious task. The environment in which the work is performed is as important as the training and the nurturing you provide.

Choose the Right Materials

"People Building" begins with the hiring process. Identification of skill precedes placement. Skills should dictate placement. The criteria for the NFL's Cowboys becoming "America's Team" was predicated on right choices. The team originally built on identifying the best athlete, and then placing them where they could most effectively contribute to the team effort.

Great emphasis is placed on credentialing, experience, and job interview skills. Rightfully so, these are important decision making factors, but they do not ensure success. The meticulous attention given the hiring procedure can include probing questions to identify strengths, and still be disappointing, or fail to produce the desired results. Getting the right person is what the interview is all about.

Helping individuals discover their "niche" requires the leader to understand that everyone is unique and diverse. The complexities of our technological society seem to be an impediment to young people in the selection of career paths. The marvels of the "information highway" in our computerized world have bewildered some in their search for career identity.

Any structure you build is only as strong as the configuration of its components. The components must be strategically placed. Each has a prescribed function that contributes to the structure's overall beauty, usefulness, and strength.

An Intangible Asset

Each staff person must be recognized as an intangible asset. Time and energy spent in development and retention are investments from which long-term dividends can be realized. Avoid needless turnover. Be sure turnover is never a leadership integrity issue. Workable, long tenured work relationships are always based on a good mix of integrity and common sense. Financial reward is not always the culprit. Job satisfaction, which includes an opportunity for personal and private growth, is also paramount. The dynamics of today's volatile work force will demand resourcefulness from tomorrow's leaders.

The emphasis on personal career objectives and corporate movement of management staff has altered previous conceptions on tenure. Five year planning strategies were reduced to three, then two, and now a year or less.

"Anyone who says businessmen deal in facts, not fiction, has never read old five-year projections."

—Malcolm Forbes

Technology and the information age has forever changed our world. Employment tenures are, as well, abbreviated. Seldom are life-long work relationships possible, or even desired. Prevailing complexities in this environment amplify risk factors. These facts serve to emphasize the importance of the need for staff stability.

People Placement

Work Roles

Proper placement provides a personalized environment for growth. The right plant given the right attention in the right soil, determines the growth of the plant. Once you identify the right soil, be sure you provide proper nourishment. Competency in any organization is based on competency in the hiring process. Incompetent hiring is a warranty deed to failure. Job tenure is more often than not determined by placement.

Staff turnover is, or should be, a matter of concern for any leader. Excessive turnover is not cost effective, and is extremely disruptive to a program or organization. There is a correlation between the longevity of employees and the success of an organization. I will discuss the correlation between the longevity of an employee and the quality of leadership later. One aspect of staff turnover must be examined in the hiring and placement of an individual. Whether it's a business for profit, a human services organization, or a faith based institution, placements impact turnover.

Repeatedly, the need to rationalize turnover is echoed by disclaimers like, "They just didn't work out" or "They made too many mistakes." Excessive turnover makes a statement and ask some questions. What is the real issue? Is it the person, the system, or is it leadership? Did the person selected for the position demonstrate compatibility with the role assignment? Could competency, or demonstrated potential, support the work performance expectations of the role?

An improperly placed person can wreak havoc in any organization. The resulting misery and agitation can become aggressive, and is always contagious. Frequently, those who do not work out do so because from the start, they were placed in work roles in which they were not capable of performing

Another dynamic in turnover is that of the leader who exhausts staff members with either ineptness or inappropriate behavior. Competent staff to whom the leader is indebted for survival will eventually tire of the lack of leadership, misrepresentations, deceitfulness, or other intolerable actions. They will choose to move on once they determine there is no end to established dysfunctional patterns.

These leaders cycle staff to retain their position. They privately and publicly profess these moves are good for the organization and "fresh blood" is needed. "Fresh blood" is good if leadership is not hemorrhaging. If it is, "fresh blood" is a cop-out for the leader. Good people become only fruit to be consumed in a perpetual fruit basket turnover.

A viable process to identify personality types, and discern their respective strengths will result in hiring wisely, and appropriately placing employees. Stringent hiring policies, and the right to privacy, prevents employers from asking scarcely more than name, rank, and serial number. For the sake of our examination of the role of "horse sense," we will focus on the leader's competency to identify personality traits and related strengths. This does not imply that everyone will succeed in every placement, but it will improve the odds.

The decision maker is disadvantaged because there are too many variables and legal prohibitions to make valuable inquiries. Since this is the case, caution is even more important, and the leader should strive to develop competent job placement skills. This is true in any organizational role, whether the organization is a profit or non-profit entity with hired or volunteer staff. Too many persons with "value added" potential have been lost by organizations because hiring skills did not support the assigned task.

Observations

Staff movement and staff retention, especially in organizations where staff were exposed to adverse circumstances, stimulated my interest. I observed a correlation between the success of long-term leaders and their ability to retain long-term staff. The basic premise for long-term staff retention is leadership skill. This encompasses hiring, placement, and the ability to create an enjoyable work environment. Placement vulnerabilities must be understood and explored. My encounter with a "common sense" approach to job placement provided insight that was never found in the best of publications on staff retention. I only regret that proper credit cannot be given the originator of the concept.

Comfort Zones

The concept consisted of a process to use "common sense" discernment to appropriately place individuals in their comfort zone. It is not a prescriptive process, it is a preventive one. It does not address particular job requirements, credentialing, experience, or other related employment issues. All of these employment requirements are facilitated by formal hiring procedures. This is a practical approach that identifies individuals by comfort zones for work performance.

Steward or Servant Role?

History is replete with the acknowledgement of societal roles and caste systems in all civilizations, past and present. Many of these civilizations were built by, and sustained by, the roles performed by servants and stewards. They constituted the infrastructure for those civilizations that relied on their abilities and labor. They labored under duress due to the abuses they endured. Some have entailed horrific accounts of human suffering and grief based on their roles.

In no way should the analogy suggest an endorsement of, or be misconstrued to suggest stereotypes. The focus of this section is the comfort level an individual will have with a role. It is not a race issue; it is a role issue. For the sake of this discussion, we will examine those abilities that are compatible to the performance of these two roles.

The roles of servants and stewards were usually obligatory. Biblical accounts placed slaves in the roles of stewards. They were placed in charge of households and had responsibility for the entire household, but owned nothing. Their selection was predicated on individual potential and demonstrated competencies. Every society has servant and stewardship roles. Again I emphasize, there is no place for preconceived stereotypes in this process.

All organizations, if successful, must have individuals that demonstrate the ability to successfully perform in these two comfort zones. The key is placement! Never assign a steward's role to one that is only qualified for, and comfortable with a servant's role. Likewise, never assign a servant's role to one qualified to be a steward. In either case, both will fail. Failure is not the fault of either. The fault solely rests with the person making the assignments.

I feel compelled to preface the following remarks with an important disclaimer. I am not remotely suggesting a published or publicized hiring policy. I am only recommending a practical application of "common sense" in the hiring interview process.

Let's examine closely the two performance comfort zones. The discipline you have exercised as a student of people now becomes your most important ally. I have noted parenthesized examples. The examples are for clarification only. Remember, all examples are replete with exceptions.

There are three prevailing differences that distinguish the priorities of a steward from those of a servant:

1. A steward will attend to details without detailed instructions. (They shine their shoes!)

2. A steward will have a preoccupation with the urgency of prompt attention to financial obligations, fiscal accountability, and personal commitments. (They pay their bills!)

3. A steward will be supersensitive and overly cautious with the possessions of others when they are in his or her care. (They respect the property of others!)

The apostle Paul reminded Christians in Corinth, that it is required of stewards that a man be found faithful, implying evidentiary qualities.

Personalized Training

This is not to suggest that individuals who find a comfort zone in the servant's role are not conscientious, honest, and attentive to task. It is to emphasize that priorities may differ. Let me illustrate. Should I direct a steward to clean one bathroom and a servant to clean another, I would have an obligation to provide meaningful instruction to both. The instruction I would provide the one would differ from the other and would be compatible to the comfort zone of each.

My instruction to the servant would require specific details. The task would be visually described for each fixture in the bathroom. Each task for the cleaning of the bathroom would be explained accordingly. "Take the spray cleaner and spray the sink and fixtures. Use this specific brush to scrub the sink until it is clean. After the sink is clean rinse the sink and fixtures with water, then dry them with a clean towel." My leadership role would require me to thoroughly define my expectations for each task in the cleaning of the bathroom. Once a thorough explanation of duties is provided, and the servant understands the assignment, the servant is prepared to repeat the process in the assigned work role. The servant is not responsible for failure if he or she did not receive adequate preparation to perform the task.

Now let's examine the steward. My instruction to the steward would be simply, "Clean the rest room." The steward would recognize the assignment as a challenge to utilize personal ingenuity and his or her expertise to accomplish the anticipated outcome. The steward, without need of definition, will assume detailed responsibilities. The steward's job description will include, "Latitude for independent judgment." Initiative and insight distinguishes the work of the steward. This is a steward's comfort zone. The steward's role says, "Assign me a task and I'll do it, but don't micromanage me." A servant's comfort zone requires greater support and input. The role doesn't burden the individual with undefined expectations. The servant's role says, "Tell me what you want me to do and how to do it, and I'll do it."

Micromanagers treat all subordinates as servants. Neither the servant nor the steward requires micromanagement. If trained properly, the servant can perform independently. If micromanaged, they are robbed of their dignity, and the leader reveals a lack of ability to make wise choices in the hiring process. If a steward is micromanaged, resentment breeds contempt, and the leader reveals leadership insecurities.

Superior Performance is the Issue

All individuals have their own personality traits that make them uniquely different. All respond differently to motivational techniques and leadership styles, but inherent values define comfort zones for work performance. The use of the analogy of a steward or servant to define specific work roles has been used to stimulate insight. It should be used to identify comfort zones, but under no circumstances should it ever be used to label individuals. Some are more comfortable in a leadership role, while others prefer a supportive role.

Under no circumstances should the intent of such a process be misconstrued to indicate superior or subservient roles. Both are equally important, and both are invaluable to any organization. If you succeed as a leader you must respect and focus on developing both roles with the same intensity. Your organization cannot operate without properly trained individuals that desire to work in the comfort zone of a capable servant. The servant's challenge may be mundane to the steward, but the steward could never perform his or her role without the support of the servant role. Without the steward's performance, there would be no role for the servant. Both are interdependent. Your management style should include an understanding of the two roles. If you give detailed instructions to a steward, he or she will resent it. A servant will expect it!

Identifying Comfort Zones

The role determination is not made at the Human Resources Office level. This determination is made in the interview process in a one-on-one relationship. The traditional rigidities of a formal employment interview must diminish at this stage in the process. Formalities do not provide the environment needed to "get acquainted" with the individual being interviewed. I am not persuaded, in today's litigious society, that we can afford the luxury of hiring individuals before we have insight into their perceptions, wants, desires, motivations, values, and priorities. You cannot effectively place individuals without insight. The right to privacy, which we all cherish and do not want infringed upon, burdens the hiring process and causes organizations to be "blindsided" because they are blindly making personnel selections.

A Cautionary Word

This process, if misused, will label individuals. Your sensitivity to this flaw is critical. The conscious or subconscious fixation of a label on any employee under any circumstance will prejudice you in your leadership role. More will be said later in this section on prejudices. A label dehumanizes, limits potential, and stigmatizes. It will always misrepresent the truth about a person. Focus your attention on the comfort zone. Use the approach as an assessment process to place individuals in positions that will allow them to be productive and grow. I contend job satisfaction is well served by the process.

I must warn you, your susceptibility to label individuals is greater than you think. Human nature is disposed to the injustice, and history substantiates the fact. Society's contentious rhetoric over the issue affirms its existence. The society-at-large is inclined to label individuals. It finds expression in faith traditions, ethnic groups, cultures, values, and political persuasions. Contrary to denials by religious entities, those that claim to be politically correct, and the national news media, all to a greater or lesser degree, engage in the practice. To the shame of all, it is most often used to promulgate a bias. This is based on our innate assumption that we fall into an elitist class that is convinced our views, insights, and conclusions are infallible. Superiority reigns!

Individuals are grouped because of their sameness. Intentionally or unintentionally, we succumb to a practice that labels individuals that are different from us. Labeling is a companion to prejudices. The truth of the matter is, all are prejudiced based on our affinity to be drawn to others that embrace what we believe or look like we look.

Servant Spirit Leadership

I want to briefly examine another caveat to the servant role. Let's turn the coin over to explore servant leadership. Leaders should demonstrate a servant's spirit. Servant leadership is nothing new. It is a precedent for leadership in the lessons Christ taught his twelve followers. The message was repeatedly taught and reinforced shortly before his death. The inevitability of self-importance had to be addressed if those he mentored continued his work in his absence.

Opportunistically, he seized the moment after observing his last Passover with them. The event was preceded by a contentious debate between his followers as to who was the greatest. His rebuttal to the absurdity of the debate was visually depicted in a pungent object lesson. He, to their amazement, became a servant, took a towel, knelt before them, and began to wash their feet. The message was clear. You cannot lead unless you serve! Servant leadership engenders dedication, devotion, and commitment to the cause. It demands respect for the leader. The genuineness of these outcomes ratify leadership.

A word of caution is appropriate. Servants are not allergic to work. The good servant establishes a precedent for performance. Leaders that exempt themselves from work create a superficial compliance standard for those they supervise. The messages are clear, "Do no more than you have to do." and "The task at hand is an obligation, not an opportunity."

History is replete with leaders who suffered defeat because followers were compelled to follow. It also records phenomenal achievements by committed minorities led by servant leaders. True servant leadership identifies with those that are led. Servant leaders do not encounter the "I am their leader and there they go" syndrome. If servant leadership is an act, and not fact, all will know.

Shop Wisely

I have never comprehended the allocated fifteen, thirty-minute, or even one-hour assembly line interview routine. In the corporate world, business transactions of large sums may exchange hands in a brief period of time, based on the restraints of time-driven decisions. These risks are not necessary in a typical personnel interview.

Typically, most leaders do not finalize a fifty to a one hundred thousand dollar purchase in thirty minutes or an hour. Time is required to assess the marketable value of the product. When you hire, you're purchasing a big-ticket item that has both benefits and liability potential. Calculate salary and benefit packages for just one year, and you'll get my point. Take your time, do your consumer research, and be a good shopper. When you find a bargain, buy! This admonishment is not intended to denigrate a bargain to cheapness. I consider value a bargain. Don't procrastinate. Return buyers often settle for unmarketable goods. "Be back" shopping practices can result in missed opportunities.

An informal interview should focus on identifiable personal priorities, values, and inherent abilities. The match of charisma, ability, and the appropriate comfort zone is dynamite! Discernment is the key! One-on-one interviews with agendas that encourage free expression are crucial. Inquiries unrelated to the work activity are often more revealing than work related questions. These should not, nor cannot, intrude into personal areas of the right to privacy.

To illustrate the process, we should consider some hypothetical inquiries. Situational questions can be asked and opinions can be solicited.

- An individual can be asked what actions they would take to perform a specific assignment.
- Details can be solicited on how they perceive the tasks should be performed.

- How they feel when asked to perform an unfamiliar task provides beneficial insights.
- What apprehensions would they experience if asked to manage the estate of an elderly relative? What would they perceive their obligations to be under these circumstances?
- They can be asked to talk about what is important to them in life.
- You might inquire of them their opinion on military protocol. How important do they think it is that the military enforce dress codes requiring polished shoes and shined brass?

Simplistic inquiries are usually more productive. The possibilities are endless, but the questions should be designed to provide insight into comfort zones. Be creative! Use your imagination.

"Blow torches" will, with time, blow the smoke away. "Give a person enough rope, and they will hang themselves." Give the individual time to talk. It takes dialogue to discern inconsistencies. The more they talk, the greater your insight. The most hazardous pitfall of the interview process is the compelling urgency to exaggerate successes. This leads to the mind-set that overstated qualifications are the norm, and validates the practice as acceptable. The resume' process encourages exaggeration and misrepresentations. Time for conversation will permit you the opportunity to more effectively evaluate truth and identify discrepancies.

If a person has seen it all, done it all, and knows it all, it should raise a "red flag" of concern. This person will not be a team player, will be pre-occupied with personal agendas, will not generally have the required skill level, and may, or may not, be compatible with organizational growth. The greater the verbiage, the more likely the expectation. Forget time! The time you invest will determine your dividends.

"There is more to some people than meets the eye." This acknowledgement could be interpreted to imply favorable or unfavorable traits. "You can't judge a book by its cover" suggests cosmetics may or may not reflect content. Both comments capture an important "heads-up" for the interviewer. Every individual has a history that is open to the interpretation of others. This increases the value of the time invested in the hiring process. Doubts created by histories can disqualify excellent candidates. Appearance can embellish credentials, misrepresent qualities, and shroud in secrecy destructive motives or mind-sets.

The irony of this dilemma is portrayed in an article circulated on the Internet entitled:

"Pastoral Search Committee"

In our search for a suitable pastor, the following scratch sheet was developed for your perusal. Of the candidates investigated by the committee, only one was found to have the necessary qualities. The list contains the names of the candidates and comments on each, should you be interested in investigating them further for future pastoral placements.

- Noah: He has 120 years of preaching experience, but no converts.
- Moses: He stutters; and his former congregation says he loses his temper over trivial things.
- Abraham: he took off to Egypt during hard times. We heard that he got into trouble with the authorities and then tried to lie his way out.
- David: He has an unacceptable moral character. He might have been considered for minister of music had he not 'fallen.'
- Solomon: He has a reputation for wisdom but fails to practice what he preaches.
- Elijah: He proved to be inconsistent, and is known to fold under pressure.
- Hosea: His family life is in shambles; divorced, and remarried to a prostitute.
- Jeremiah: He is too emotional, alarmist; some say a real 'pain in the neck.'
- Amos: Comes from a farming background; better off picking figs.
- John: He says he is a Baptist, but lacks tact and dresses like a hippie; would not feel comfortable at a church potluck supper.
- Peter: Has a bad temper, and was heard to have even denied Christ publicly.
- Paul: We found him to lack tact. He is too harsh. His appearance is contemptible, and he preaches too long.
- Timothy: He has potential, but is too young for the position.

- Jesus: He tends to offend church members with his preaching, especially Bible scholars. He is also too controversial. He even offended the search committee with his pointed questions.
- Judas: He seemed to be very practical, co-operative, good with money, cares for the poor, and dresses well. We all agreed that he is just the man we are looking for to fill the vacancy as our Senior Pastor.

Thank you for all you have done in assisting us with our pastoral search.

Sincerely,
The Pastoral Search Committee

Supervision Placements

An Awesome Responsibility

The responsibility to place people in supervisory positions is an awesome trust. Your credibility is at stake. The sensitivity you demonstrate toward staff that will be under the supervision of a person you hire is a character issue. It speaks volumes about your personal principles and ethics. The hiring of someone that will have authority or control over the lives of others is a moral responsibility. Carelessness prevails when hasty decisions are predicated on convenience, immediate profit, friendships, political payoffs, or credentialing needs. Your choice will affect the lives of every person under the direction of the supervisor you hire. This is too important for trial and error.

Be Sensitive to References With Ulterior Motives

Meaningful work references should be pursued before individuals are placed in leadership roles. "Meaningful" doesn't mean handpicked references, or persons selected because of their political power and community clout. Supervisory roles have been used as payment for political IOUs, or favoritisms for close friends.

Be cognizant of the fact that individuals from other organizations that have little or no knowledge of your organization, will provide you

with reports on requested work references.
Two considerations must be entertained.

1. Their report is based on their knowledge of the individual's performance in their work setting and/or supervisory role.
2. The responsibility to determine the impact the individual's demeanor, skills, and personality will have on the position and your organization is placed solely on the hiring entity.

Some employers, in the referral process, opportunistically seize the moment to rid themselves of unproductive or problematic supervisors by providing fabricated recommendations. The temptation to expedite the resolution to a personnel issue by relocating the individual, without undesired personnel action, can be appealing. In actuality, truth can only be obtained at the "grass roots" level. If you want the absolute truth about an individual's leadership skills, ask those that have been supervised by the individual.

Beware of Chronic Destructive Behaviors!

Our grandparents referred to these individuals as those who have "bad blood." These were those who had bad reputations in the community due to their chronic misbehaviors. Perhaps the analogy should be remembered when job applicants have a chronic history of disruptive behaviors. Placement of an individual in a leadership role with a known history of, or observation of, potential disruptive behaviors is inexcusable. The hiring of known antagonists and troublemakers has been justified by some leaders because the perpetrators had either academic credentials, experience, or expertise that the leader perceived would be a personal asset to embellish their own stature.

> "You don't set a fox to watching the chickens just because he has a lot of experience in the hen house."
> —Harry Truman

Delusionary thinkers, in leadership roles, believe they are especially endowed with skills to supervise those that others have been unable to supervise. Don't be overwhelmed by your ego to believe that you possess uncanny leadership qualities to alter chronic behavioral patterns. These patterns include an array of behaviors and personalities: the obnoxious braggart, the "know it all," the individual with a history of moral indiscretions, the one that has demonstrated abusive behaviors, and the ineffective or incompetent manager.

"Keep the bull out of the china cabinet." People can be fragile when subjected to, and placed in a position of submission to destructive behavioral patterns or personalities. People are priceless, living commodities. They deserve to be treated with dignity and respect. They must be handled with care. Destructive leadership personalities have the potential to destroy people. It would be as apropos to have "the fox guard the chicken coop" as it would be to place your staff in harms way. An irresponsible job placement will always result in negative consequences.

"Authority without wisdom is like a heavy ax without an edge, fitter to bruise than polish."
—Anne Bradstreet, American author

"Treat people
as if they were
what they ought to be
and
you help them
to become
what they are
capable
of becoming."
—Johann Wolfgang von Goethe

CHAPTER 5

PEOPLE NEEDS

People Need Leadership

I am convinced people want competent leadership; they respect it, and will respond to it. A wise leader will value people and use things. A self-serving leader will use people and value things.

Boss Or Leader?

...A Boss	...A Leader
...Drives	...Leads
...Relies on Authority	...Relies on Cooperation
...Says "I"	...Says "We"
...Creates Fear	...Creates Confidence
...Knows How	...Shows How
...Creates Resentment	...Breeds Enthusiasm
...Fixes Blame	...Fixes Mistakes
...Makes Work Drudgery	...Makes Work Interesting

—Source Unknown

Leadership Is Not Lordship

Dictators

My generation witnessed the aftermath of dictatorships on an international scale. The international scene during World War II was dominated by dictators. The post war attempts to appease them made it worse. This led to lingering consequences that have been apparent in our present generation. Until recent years, dictators were the rule and not the exception. This international mindset subtly permeated our own societal culture. It found expression in diverse leadership roles. Political leadership

81

roles assumed an aura of unquestioned authority that entitled them to lifestyles that were extravagant and abusive. Autocratic leadership always leads to extravagancies. Privileges entitled them to a "hands-off" posture even by the media. The "trickle down" affect was evident in the work place. "Bosses" had power and used it. Injustices spawned labor union movements to cope with these oppressive practices. Subordinates were abused and misused. Ministerial roles were even impacted. Pastoral leadership was autocratic. The rigidity of control dictated lifestyles based on unquestioned, opinionated interpretations of religious practice. There was an expectation on the part of the general public that they would be told what to do and how to do it. Opportunistic egos were obliged to capitalize on this susceptibility. A selfish application of authority and knowledge made the general public subservient to dictatorial practices.

"People can be led...not driven." Dictatorial leadership conjures up images of sweatshops and antiquated bosses. Intimidation to some is an art. This style of leadership is dysfunctional. It is frequently an exercise to disguise inexperience or inadequate leadership skills. The boss façade feeds on egotistical motivations and smoke screens a lack of confidence in one's own capability to perform as a leader. An inferiority complex and the inability to privately engage in confrontational corrective measures have also resulted in public displays of bold rebukes to bolster self-images.

"You can win the battle and lose the war" when perceived mandates or coercions become a rule of practice. The story of Johnny and his first day at school may provide insight. Johnny was certainly not accustomed to the strange new rule that restrained him to the confines of his chair for, what he perceived to be, an unacceptable period of time. He concluded the old behavioral patterns were more desirable and accommodating. This being the case, he took unapproved liberties to wander about the classroom at will. By early afternoon, the teacher was totally exhausted by her futile efforts to keep Johnny seated at his desk. Exasperated, she took Johnny by the hand, led him to his chair, firmly placed both hands on his shoulder and guided him to a seated position. The action was accompanied by a stern command that he would stay seated at his desk until the school day closed. As she turned to walk away, she overheard Johnny's comment to a friend seated adjacent to him. "I may be sitting down on the outside, but I am standing up on the inside." People may permit a leader to drive them, but they will not mentally consent to it. Action without inspired consent is unproductive.

People will eventually leave their assigned chair, and there will be adverse consequences for the leader.

"The chickens always come home to roost." People can be intimidated, driven, abused, and misused, but the final chapter will always have an unpleasant ending. Even though the ordeal for subordinates may seem unbearably long, the behavior will usually ensure an exit visa for the abusive leader.

Individuals not normally given to retaliation or retribution, if intentionally harassed, embarrassed, or abused have the potential to participate in the demise of the perpetrator. A television commercial advertising punctual car maintenance contains a veiled threat, "I'll get you now or get you later." A leader who subscribes to a dictatorial leadership style can expect retaliation. When you allow your ego to violate the ego of another, you guarantee a negative outcome. Facilitate don't dictate.

The stereotype of "boss" is more than demonstrative behaviors and verbose language. The negative connotation is more intrusive than mere imagery. The behaviors noted in the comparison of bosses and leaders include subtle autocratic practices. These are dealt with in differing formats in the book.

Share Knowledge

I want to focus on another subtle dynamic. Autocratic leaders use knowledge to bolster their morale and strengthen their control. The subversion of, or control of knowledge, can sustain their retention of power. Dictatorial behavior and menacing language are not the only indicators of autocratic leadership. Knowledge deficits are just as oppressive. Knowledge energizes freedom. It demands authenticity from the leader and requires accountability.

"Knowledge is power." It is also true, "Power can corrupt." Authoritarian knowledge control promulgates elitism that can be, and has been, abusive. Control is used to intimidate. The goal is unquestioned authority. "Old habits die hard" and "Absolute power corrupts absolutely."

The dissemination of knowledge has changed the leadership role. "The clock will never be turned back." "The genie is out of the bottle." Leadership has a new challenge. The leader that will share knowledge, demonstrate a desire to learn, and is not threatened by those that are more knowledgeable, will create a learning environment. The creation of a learning environment encourages growth. The disciplined leader who learns to direct the wisdom of others is the leader that will meet the needs of those that are led. Leadership that self-servingly hordes knowledge and spurns the wisdom of others will be short lived.

Seek Knowledge

A wise leader benefits from, learns from, and depends on the expertise of those being led. Learn to trust the wisdom of those that have demonstrated superb insight, wisdom, and expertise. The ability to creatively utilize the wisdom of others requires intellectualized leadership. Intellectual leadership has direction, and the ability to communicate that course of direction. One has to know where they're going if they are to arrive at their destination. People are sensitive to, and will immediately detect, a lack of direction. The skill level of a leader is measured by the leader's ability to unleash the potential of those he or she leads.

Value unembellished wisdom. When seeking counsel, remember excessive verbiage does not equate to extensive knowledge. Garrulous individuals may be more talk than substance. More often than not, excessive verbiage is proof positive of self-perceived deficits in one's life experience. Leaders are often misled by poor counsel. This subject is discussed more fully later in the book in the section titled "Advice."

The leader must be a student, ever learning, and well prepared for the task. An admirable learning goal should include a firm commitment to obtain a comprehensive knowledge of every aspect of the organization he or she leads. This knowledge allows the leader greater insight to evaluate input provided by advisors or consultants. The learning process will be impaired if the leader projects a know-it-all approach to leadership, or subsequently attempts to be deceitful regarding his or her knowledge base. All sorts of misrepresentations, manipulations, and distortions have been creatively used to deceive subordinates. The fact is, they easily discern these cover-ups, and the leader's respect is sacrificed on the altar of their own personal vanity.

Insecure leaders that attempt to bolster their public image will either superimpose perceptions of their own wisdom on the wisdom of others, or plagiarize the expertise of others. They will seek to associate with knowledgeable professionals to impress them with misrepresentations of their own credentials. Don't embellish what you don't understand. Pretense without substance is a full disclosure of leadership insecurity. Don't misuse the wisdom of others. Embrace it, encourage it, and enlist it.

Another incongruity is the leader that intentionally seeks individuals that have skills and wisdom inferior to their own. These leaders lack confidence in their skill level and can be tempted to seek out unqualified individuals. Usually the practice is disguised as being an exercise to develop people. Be honest! The real motive is obvious. Unqualified people do not present a threat, and they can be controlled to accommodate self-serving purposes. The real issue is control. Leadership releases, it doesn't control.

In Summary...

The mystery of human behavior consistently offers surprises and stimulates intriguing unanswerable questions. This is true in the frequent use of two of the least effective and most obvious of all deceptions.

1. Excesses: The temptation to use excessive verbiage or create "busy work" to smoke screen a lack of knowledge only serves to exaggerate incompetence. Remember, smoke screens dissipate quickly. These deceptions are self-deceptions. These are used as a ploy to impress those that are being led with a misperception of an unattained skill level by the leader. It is a revealing disclosure of personal inadequacies and an obvious lack of direction. A lack of direction by an image builder will generate nonsense work for subordinates. Productivity suffers when individuals are burdened with "busy work." The leader who succumbs to these temptations must ask, "Can I afford the luxury of my own vanity?"

2. Egoisms: "They are bigger when they are hatched than at any other time." A novice mesmerized by a degree of success and driven by egotistical motives can be hurtful to people. People become stepping-stones as opposed to building blocks in the organization. Ego is an infectious factor. Our parents have reminded us, "You never fly so high but what you have to come down." As a young man, I was given a definition of ego I have never forgotten. "Ego is the hypodermic God allows a man to administer to himself to prove to that man what a fool he really is." It has also been suggested, "There is no smaller package than a person wrapped up in him or her self." Unshared, misused, or abusive use of knowledge may suggest an ego is out of control. "Don't toot your own horn!"

People Need Empowerment

An effective leader must know how to delegate. Delegate without strings. Often leaders profess to delegate, and even go through the motion of delegating, but operate as if they have all the answers. Delegated responsibilities are often used as a subterfuge. If you adopt this style, expect resentment. The more competent the worker, the greater the resentment will be. This practice is a fast track to failure. The loss of respect of your most knowledgeable people will have subtle consequences that will eventually undermine your ability to lead competent people. Don't "second-guess" those to whom you delegate responsibility to. Rely on their competence and refrain from becoming an "armchair quarterback."

Be a good steward of your delegation authority. Never misuse it. Laziness is a stigma, whether present in the life of the leader or the follower. Laziness, couched in delegation, will reproduce. Inactivity by the leader can lead to mischievousness, deception, and distortion. "An idle mind is the devil's workshop."

People Need Effective Communication

Keep It Simple

There have been more misunderstandings due to faulty communication than any other organizational shortfall. Say what you mean and mean what you say. Say it in the right way, say it at the right place, and say it at the right time. A departure from either can create hard feelings and undesired consequences. It is especially important to say what you actually mean regarding problematic difficulties.

An attempt to be coy or convey hidden messages in public or private discourses may provide a temporary reprieve, but will not resolve any issue. In fact, it allows the perceived problem to become more complex and raises the anxiety level of all involved parties. Subtle messages designed to deliver subliminal messages are a cop-out. They should never be used as a leadership directive or process to resolve a difficult situation. Never assume that people understand your communication. Inquire and remember the "KISS" rule, "Keep it simple stupid!"

Don't be snared with the temptation to impress your listeners with your knowledge, philosophy, or expertise. If you have either, they will know it! If you have neither and verbalize a proverbial "snow job," they will know that too, and will resent it. The quickest way to lose a listener is to insult their intelligence.

"The Devil is in the Details"

Communication must be decisive and unencumbered by subtleties or subterfuge when providing reports on the status of your organization. Inattentive governing boards victimized by this deceit will be both attentive and vindictive when embarrassed by their own oversight. Communication requiring misleading verbiage to conceal a detrimental truth is exploitation. It is predicated on premeditated misrepresentations usually disguised in implied truths and unstated realities. Undisclosed details can be harmful. Deception always seems to have the capability to surface and expose the perpetrator. Don't practice deception, and avoid the inevitable!

Public or Private

"Praise in public, counsel in private." Common sense demands sensitivity. Issues requiring communication, whether praise or admonishment, must be discreetly addressed. A violation of this courtesy will always result in irreparable breaches of confidence. Public praise and recognition strengthens relationships, builds morale, and reinforces personal worth. Public rebuke or counsel is demeaning, cowardly, and crudely insensitive.

The life of the communication experience is a reflection of the importance one should ascribe to it. The life of public counsel or rebuke is without end for the individual affected by it, based on the dynamics or intensity of the encounter. The life of public recognition may end, but positive outcomes extend beyond its memory. Private counsel nurtures the admonition process and can have a long lasting influence on the recipient.

Document, Document, Document!

When communication involves delegating or directives, document the interaction, write it down, date it, copy it, have both parties sign it, and file it. A written record makes it official and prevents unnecessary misunderstandings.

Communication to delegate responsibility must be clear. It cannot be presented as suggestions, possibilities, or considerations. Leaders who are reticent to distinctly verbalize directives send mixed messages and confuse the listener. Directives leaving the impression follow-up action is contingent on either endorsement or personal discretion, will usually get the lack of attention they deserve.

Expectations can only be understood when effectively communicated. When verbal communication is used for either correction or instruction, one important rule should be adhered to. How you say it is as important as what you say. Correction requires constructive communication and the instruction given requires that the information be relevant.

People Need Positive Reinforcement

The Need

A tenured leader told me he did not believe in positive reinforcement. He rationalized that job satisfaction was adequate reinforcement, especially in any human services occupation. He obviously never learned the virtue of consistency. I do not ever recall observing him refuse personal praise, recognition, or remuneration for his work. He was always willing to be more than adequately compensated for his own services, while minimizing the value of rewards for those responsible for his success. The outcomes produced by his leadership provided evidence that negates his theory.

All top performers need reinforcement, but some need it more than others. Reinforcement unleashes potential. Reinforcement engenders respect. Rationalizations for a failure to provide appropriate reinforcement are only acknowledgements of derelict oversights.

Selfishness argues, "You create greater demands for financial compensation if praise is given to top performers." Contrarily, I would argue the opposite is true. If reinforcement is proper and truthful, it creates greater job satisfaction and diminishes preoccupations with increased salary and benefits. Praise and recognition will have a positive impact on the budget of any organization. Positive reinforcement may be the greatest bargain in today's economy. It has a proven record of being cost effective.

No Substitute for Adequate Compensation

Rewards are important! Recognition is good, but rewards are better.

Research has verified that rewards do not necessarily have to be of a financial nature to be effective. It contends individuals desire recognition of good performance and the opportunity to professionally advance. It argues that individuals remember rewards long after they have forgotten additional financial compensation. The analogy of carrots has been widely circulated to depict rewards. The analogy has been taken so literally by some, the rewards equate to little more than a carrot. Carrots are good, but supplemental sweetness makes them taste better.

I believe a comment on the research is appropriate. Plaques and special events are not common place in a person's life. This fact alone facilitates recall. Financial rewards are not as easily remembered because financial compensation is a routine event in life. We exchange increments of our life for compensation, if we are employed. The two dynamics are clear. First, financial compensation is routine, and secondly, discretionary use of money as a reward diminishes remembrance.

Even though long-term memory may not recall the amount of financial remuneration, it does not moderate the importance of the positive impact it will have on the recipient. This is especially true for the employee that struggles to buy the necessities of life. The individual struggling to buy bread may not have an office wall upon which to display his or her ego. They certainly will not find a piece of paper in a frame, or an imprinted plaque, as important as food and clothes for their children.

Positive reinforcement is not to be used as substitutionary compensation. Stinginess, like generosity, will be reciprocated. The leader that unselfishly cares about the welfare of subordinates will develop unselfish subordinates that, of their own volition, will sacrifice time and energy for the success of the organization. A proper mix of praise and pay has the potential to make great things happen!

> "Pay your people the least possible and you'll get from them the same."
>
> —Malcolm Forbes, publisher

Doing without does not equate to dedication. Expectations that subordinates should sacrifice adequate compensation to demonstrate their dedication to their work role is an absurdity. Leaders enjoying lucrative compensation packages and perks should be the first to advocate for those who have made them successful. It is blatant hypocrisy if a leader is chintzy with others, while obsessed with his or her own exorbitant salary objectives.

Use Rewards Wisely

Don't carelessly give them. Rewards work! Horses respond to sugar cubes and treats. As a teenager, I would carry treats in my pocket to simplify getting my horse out of the pasture. It always worked. Mishandled rewards don't work! Even though reinforcements are effective, they can be misused and can also be counterproductive. This is just another reason for the leader to be a student of people.

Careless, excessive use of praise becomes meaningless and cheap. A friend of mine purchased a young bull to service some Longhorns we had jointly purchased. Our pride and excitement over the bull's potential caused us to carelessly and excessively use feeding cubes. We anticipated it would make our work easier and the bull less aggressive if we placated the bull with treats. It didn't work! After a period of time, the bull's expectations created serious problems for us when we were in the lot with him. We learned an invaluable lesson. The appropriate use of rewards is as important as the sincerity of the reward. The analogy is flawed, due to the fact we did have an ulterior motive, but hopefully it conveys my message. Reinforcement must be appropriate and genuine. Know your people, know what energizes them, and learn the disciplines of positive reinforcement.

A pat on the back is always appreciated. Someone has suggested a pat on the back is just four vertebras removed from a kick in the pants. Your leadership will be more effective if you move up four vertebras.

Be sure they are appropriate.

Reward systems should inspire, elevate, and be age appropriate. Habilitation for individuals with mental retardation focuses on age appropriateness, This respects the dignity of the individual, while introducing the individual to new objectives for personal growth.

This value appears lost in a recent new approach to rewards. Point systems now being promulgated either reward individuals with points or penalize them with point reductions. The number of accumulated points then determines raise potential in annual evaluations. The workplace is not a kindergarten or elementary classroom. The age level of the exercise is demeaning and juvenile. The workplace has moved beyond Dr. Spock, children's games, and dunce caps.

People Need Love

The reader's response may be, "Now you've gone too far! I don't have to love people to lead people." Now that I have your attention, I'll make my point. The word "love" in our vocabulary means all things to all people. The word is inadequate to express the diverse emotional expressions claiming its use. Love is more clearly defined in the Greek language.

In scriptural context the extent of the emotional affection expressed is defined by the choice of the word that is used. Two such frequently used words will illustrate my point; "agape" speaks of a sacred love, whereas "phileo" alludes to a mere expression of fondness. People need to know that you personally care about them and their welfare. It has been suggested that "love" is an elastic word. The degree of commitment you receive from subordinates will equate to the perception they have of your concerns for them.

A Discipline

I remember hearing the report of a greatly maligned minister who succinctly described his feelings regarding his ministerial duties. He said, "I love to preach, but I can't stand people!" Introspection by another minister encountering similar difficulties and the spontaneity of his anger led him to declare, "I have made up my mind; I am going to love every damn one of them!" After having time to reflect on these emotional outbursts, I've concluded, both captured the exasperation of "unconditional love."

The Bible, whose message they expounded, has, what appears to be, an outlandish command. The command is, "Love your enemies, and do good to them that despitefully use you...!" The command is sacred and divine, but the responsibility is human. Let's not be naïve or pious, it's not easy, or natural, to love your enemies. Truth demands an acknowledgement. If we are to succeed in loving an enemy, it will require discipline. The older I get, the more I'm convinced, that love, regardless of its usage, is a discipline. Discipline is a choice of the will. The divine aspect of "people love" is observed of Christ in His garden prayer and in His cry from the cross. "Father, forgive them, for they know not what they do!" If you love the unlovely, it requires discipline. Love, as a verb, denotes action.

"People are unreasonable, illogical, and self-centered.
Love them anyway.

If you do good, people will accuse you of selfish motives.
Do good anyway.

If you are successful, you will win false friends and true enemies.
Succeed anyway.

Honesty and frankness make you vulnerable.
Be honest and frank anyway.

The good you do today will be forgotten tomorrow.
Do good anyway.

The biggest people with the biggest ideas can be shot down
by the smallest people with the smallest minds.
Think big anyway.

People favor underdogs, but always follow top dogs.
Fight for some underdogs anyway.

What you spend years building may be destroyed overnight.
Build anyway.

Give the world the best you've got, and you'll be
kicked in the teeth.

Give the world the best you've got anyway."

—Dr. Robert Schuller

Two Divine Commands

Society's sordid concept of love distorts the sacred validity of its command. The message of the Bible is summarized in two great commands; the first, "Love God with all your heart and soul," and the second, "Love your neighbor as yourself." This second command is as overwhelming as the command to love your enemy. Self-love does not imply self-centeredness is endorsed in the second command. Self-centeredness and selfishness are so natural and forceful they are the primary source of society's ills. Loving your neighbor as yourself will require discipline. Loving your neighbor more than yourself requires character of an ethereal nature.

The ability to relegate self to a subservient role requires character. Character is said to be what a person is when no one is watching. It is defined as moral excellence. Morality is defined as virtue. Virtue is defined as conformity to a standard of right. The divine standard of right requires growth to achieve it. Character can be mimicked, but cannot be faked. The true character of a person will always surface. Life events will guarantee it.

Love Overcomes

Love overcomes diversity. It is the resourcefulness that allows one to overcome diversity, prejudices, and vices. The scope of its influence is rooted in its inherent attributes.

I Corinthians 13:4-8
Love...
    ...is patient
    ...is kind
    ...is never envious
    ...is not jealous
    ...is not boastful or vainglorious
    ...does not display itself haughtily
    ...is not conceited—arrogant
    ...is not inflated with pride
    ...is not rude
    ...does not act unbecomingly
    ...does not insist on its own rights
    ...is not self-seeking
    ...is not touchy, fretful, or resentful
    ...takes no account of the evil done to it
    ...pays no attention to suffered wrong
    ...does not rejoice at injustice and unrighteousness
    ...rejoices when right and truth prevail
    ...bears up under anything and everything that comes
    ...is ready to believe the best of every person

...its hopes are fadeless under all circumstances
...NEVER FAILS

—The Amplified New Testament

This perspective led me to this conclusion. You will only successfully lead those you discipline yourself to appreciate and value. I would ask you to explore this discipline. Those that follow your leadership will have to be convinced you are sincerely interested in them; their desires, their concerns, and their goals. A leadership connotation of "love" will be needed to achieve this noble goal.

"The actions of men
are
like the index
of a book...

they point out
what
is most remarkable
in them."

—Heinrich Heine

CHAPTER 6

COMMON COURTESIES

Common Misconception

"Mind your manners." Certain practices are acceptable and some are not. Most likely, if you are a student of the role of leadership, you will argue that a review of the following courtesies is unnecessary. I would like to remind you, common sense is practicing what shouldn't have to be said. Every leader with any degree of experience has been introduced to the value of, and the importance of, routine courtesies. These practices should be as normal as breathing, but empirical evidence suggests many leaders in prominent roles have yet to master the ABCs of leadership. I would like to challenge you to conduct a common sense assessment of your personal attentiveness to these oversights. I encourage you to buckle your seat belt as we get up close and personal. "If it is to be…it is up to you and me."

Persons demonstrating ill-will and grumpy attitudes may be assessed as having a "Bee in their bonnet." The inference is based on the assumption that their demeanor is a reflection of some unpleasant experience. An analogy might be beneficial to introduce us to the importance of small, but crucial courtesies. The care of the beekeeper is rewarded with honey, but if upset, the bee will sting its keeper. Likewise, the care and attention you give to the topics (Be's) in this chapter will either sweeten your leadership role or, if unattended, be an irritant in your "bonnet."

Be Punctual

It is unacceptable to be late for an appointment. It is inexcusable to be habitually late for appointments. It is self-destructive to miss appointments. A timely telephone call is an appropriate courtesy, but even this precaution, if habitually used, annuls its effectiveness. "You can only go to the well so many times before it dries up." No action is more disrespectful or inappropriate than tardiness. Some leaders are quick to rationalize, "But I'm busy." Rationalization of this nature reveals a subconscious or conscious belief that they are more important than others. The greater they perceive their accomplishments to be, the more likely it is that the infraction is chronic.

Leaders that deem punctuality as being unimportant are simply undisciplined. Some choose to jokingly excuse their behavior. Whatever the reason for the behavior, the evidence is revealing. Tardiness demonstrates a lack of respect. It ignores the needs and concerns of others. The behavior is rude, egotistical, inconsiderate, and disrespectful. Lateness, unless circumstantially unavoidable, says, "I'm important and you are not." It says, "My time is more important than yours." Chronic tardiness or failures to make appointments publicizes the fact that the leader is a poor manager of his or her time, life, and responsibilities. These habits are public billboards of rudeness and self-centeredness.

Time is money. The math is simple. If you keep sixteen people waiting for you and you are fifteen minutes late, you have wasted four hours of their time and fifteen of your own. Your tardiness as a leader can be expensive, and it doesn't impress subordinates that you are "busy." The principle of usefulness is, "If you want something done, recruit the busiest person you can locate to accomplish it." Busy people are busy because they have established a reputation. "Full plates" are the norm, not the exception. Busy folks accomplish great things and don't waste time.

Be Considerate

It is inconsiderate to monopolize conversations and overwhelm people with one's perceived brilliance, accomplishments, or philosophy. Accomplishments and brilliance, if worthy of note, will speak for themselves. The know-it-all will quickly exhaust his or her believability. The temptation to provide answers to questions that have never been asked has never impressed those worth impressing.

"It's what you learn after you know it all that really counts."

The perceived ability to provide the answer to every conceivable question based on fabricated accounts of past successes leads to self-deception.

Limited success, or the lack thereof, can stimulate the repetition of vaunted reports; to achieve, through verbiage, what was never achieved through experience. Repetition doesn't create reality, it distorts it. Distorted reality, in time, will always victimize the originator.

Those that play this game become victims of their own deceptions. Self-deception then becomes the only certification deemed necessary to coach the game they never played. "Arm chair quarterbacks" never won a ball game. "It's one thing to talk about bull fighting, it's quite another to get in the ring."

A preoccupation to convince others of our accomplishments is a testimonial of our own insecurities. Excessive talk leads to excess! Caution is advised when a leader is obsessed with excessive verbiage. The more one says, the more apt he or she will be to say what shouldn't be said. The verbose practitioner believes that truth is based on repetitious reports.

Saying something doesn't make it true; saying it often makes it obviously untrue. Credibility is earned, not self-promoted. The leader committed to being a student of people will listen more than they talk. We all have been reminded this is the reason the Lord gave us two ears and one mouth. We should spend twice as much time listening as we do talking. Respect valid experience and glean knowledge from the successes of others, but beware of believing your own or the misrepresentations of others.

Be A Good Communicator

Value Communication

Communicative conversation is a two way street. People talk because they have something they believe others should hear. Communicants value their message and input. The personal value the communicant attaches to the message demands that the listener listen with the same intensity. Each party must concentrate on being captivated by the other person's message. Selfishness short-circuits the communication process. Some go through the motion of listening while preoccupied with their own profound thoughts and planned comments. Poor listeners are poor actors.

It is selfish not to be a good listener. Those who have an audience with you deserve your undivided attention. Anything less is not acceptable. If, for some reason, the timing of an encounter is not convenient, it is more honorable to reschedule than be a derelict listener. Attentive listening is a discipline. When burdened with overwhelming responsibilities and deadlines, it is possible to hear without listening. Communication attempts by others can become little more than tolerable, or intolerable, noise.

Good listeners work at listening. Good communicators are good listeners that value and solicit information others can provide. When soliciting information, listen! Nothing is more rude than to make an inquiry of another person and then not listen to the response.

Don't interrupt while others are speaking. Comprehension always precedes an intelligent reply. Never attempt to predict, preempt, or, worse yet, go so far as to complete the sentence of the one with whom you're conversing. Any response to a partial message is likely to be an improper one. Partial truths and insights will lead to costly misunderstandings.

Eye Contact

The most important attribute of a good listener is the discipline of consistent eye contact. Eye contact focuses your attention on the speaker and prevents distractions. It honors your speaker and hones your communication skills. It allows you to interpret non-verbal communication. You not only have the opportunity to hear the communication, you also have the luxury to observe unspoken messages.

Personal or organizational success is contingent on effective communication. Learn to listen as if your life depends upon it, because professionally, it does. Ross Perot said, "My first message is: Listen, listen, listen…to the people who do the work."

Be Honest

"Some people will lie when the truth would fit better." As a youngster, I recall my mother's frequent recitation of this saying to emphasize the absurdity of some falsehoods. The truth is, the truth always fits better. In the "people business," there is no single virtue more important than truth. Relationships must be established on mutual trust. Accomplished leadership skills pale in comparison to the practice of truth by a leader. Trust is a by-product of truth. Truth is immutable.

Circumstances may change, but truth is a reliable constant. Truth is established on factual absolutes. The absence of absolutes makes anything acceptable. There are no variables, exceptions, or circumstances that give credence to a lie. Truth changed is a lie.

> "Whatever is only almost true is quite false and among the most dangerous of errors, because it is the most likely to lead astray."
> —Henry Ward Beecher

A generation ago, "a man's word was his bond." Business deals were consummated with a handshake and a promise. Dishonesty has created a litigious society shackled by "fine print" contracts designed to obscure the truth. Advertisers become "wordsmiths" to skillfully conceal the truth and misinform the public. Today's society rationalizes misrepresentations and scorns honest disclosures. Truth is devalued in the pursuit of prosperity, fame, and happiness. A lie is costly, but truth is priceless. Individuals who chronically lie fail to count the cost. Dishonesty is short lived. Sooner or later truth will always surface.

Premeditated attempts to manipulate or mislead through partially communicated messages and half-truths will always prove to be destructive to you and your organization. A partial truth is not truth. The failure to fully disclose pertinent facts is not truth. Misrepresentations can be communicated nonverbally. As we discussed in the section on "Rumor Control," a timely wink of the eye, a nod of the head, or a facial expression can be used to imply what is not true. Be sensitive to the fact that a single lie has the capability to discredit lifelong credibility. Frequent misrepresentations by a leader may achieve temporal fame or recognition, but in the long run, it will result in his or her demise. "Oh what a tangled web we weave, when at first we choose to deceive."

Never be so foolish as to feign a commitment to truth. If you do not embrace truth as absolute, you cannot be true to yourself or others. What you believe about truth will determine who you are and what you do. What you are will either testify for you or against you.

It is possible to mimic truth. It is impossible to experience the power of truth when truth is misused. Self-serving leaders crave the positive outcomes of these principles while spurning truth. Accepting truth as an absolute and acting upon it is a pre-requisite to positive outcomes. Truth is not a lucky rabbit's foot with which you adorn yourself to deceive others.

The mystery and majesty of the divine was tantalizing to one called Simon the Sorcerer. He solicited divine outcomes without adherence to divine process. He failed to understand either the source or the dynamic of divine manifestations. His energy was wasted because he failed to appropriate truth as a personal experience. Some leaders want the benefits of truth principles, but do not practice truth. They speak of truth and integrity, but practice dishonesty and deception. Their actions are destructive. Simon the Sorcerer was identified as Simon Magus in postapostolic Christian writings. He corrupted Christians in Rome with his teachings. His belief system was based on his fascination with the miraculous, not on true belief in the message of Jesus.

Adherence to truth principles does have a life of its own and does produce positive outcomes. Inherent in the principle is the outcome. This fact does not, however, encompass impure motives. The performance of the principle produces the outcome. You can benefit from practicing truth without embracing its Author. This is the essence of truth.

Jesus reminded His followers, "I am the way, the truth and the life." Mahatma Gandhi was a student of the principles taught by Jesus, but did not accept Him as the Messiah. His altruistic pursuit of these principles made him world famous as a moral leader, but not a follower of Jesus. He mobilized India to discard its dehumanizing caste system. The irony of his example is a mystery. It should certainly capture the attention of Christians who profess Jesus, but fail to practice His truth.

Be Organized

It is Important!

"A chain is no stronger than its weakest link." The leader can have leadership potential, be sincere, creative, and energetic, but fail miserably if organizational considerations are not given a priority status. If a lack of organization is your weakness, it is not an incidental shortcoming: it's an "accident waiting to happen." It will undermine your noblest dreams and visionary goals. Organization is a pre-requisite to fulfilled aspirations. Productivity and the organizational strength of any organization are predicated on the leader's organizational skills. Innovative ideas and creativity are only productive when organizational considerations are put in place to ensure fruition.

A Burden

A lack of organization is burdensome to associates and subordinates. Henry Ford introduced the assembly line to generate mass production of a product. It revolutionized manufacturing potential and ushered in a new era. Assemblers were organized in such a way that they individually contributed to the finished product. Organization determined the success of the assembly line. The success of each person was contingent on the success of others until the product left the assembly line.

The failure of one assembler would negatively impact the productivity of every one on the assembly line. One person had the potential to disrupt timelines and impact the quality of the finished product. A singular failure became a burden to every assembler. This organizational structure immediately identified any deficiency or unreliable assembler. Productivity is the outcome of organizational strength. The failure to be organized will work a hardship on those that depend on you for leadership direction. Direction determines your destination! Organizational planning focuses on a fixed destination. Planning skills will be scrutinized more closely in the section entitled, "Planning."

Fickle Failure

A leader must be able to discern if organizational planning has depth and positive long-term outcomes. A preoccupation with a "pie in the sky," "quick fix" approach to planning will not accomplish this end result. Instability on the part of the leader contributes to poor organizational planning. Some leaders operate on whims, gimmickry, and fads. Direction is determined by the latest craze, guaranteed success seminar, or best selling book on success. Be aware of the fact that it is only the author of the best selling book on success who succeeds. It has been suggested that the shortest route to riches is to write a book and entitle it, *How To Get Rich Quickly.* Instability and a lack of direction prohibit organizational planning.

Organization is more than planning sessions or impressive charts. Organization is structure. People, resources, and assets are made a cohesive whole to accomplish an end result. Planning that doesn't result in a commitment to implementation and completion does nothing for the organization. Plan completion requires time, and the recognition of this fact should be a component of the planning process. Fickle planning based on momentary whims will never achieve organizational strength.

Flaunted organizational claims are a farce if, systematically, the infrastructure does not validate the claims. Organizational claims are often little more than an organizational pretense. In such cases the organizational chart is only a paper product reflecting a figment of the imagination. Form without substance leads to unrestrained confusion.

Afterthought Planning

Leaders that persistently fail to organize and act on spontaneity find it necessary to become proficient deceivers, and find themselves in the quagmire of repeated crises. They react to self-inflicted problematic situations based on the whims and fads of the most recent seminar. The fallacy is that reactionary management would not have been necessary had they developed a proactive organizational structure to prevent and address problem areas. Insult is added to injury when the deceptive leader, after the fact, reports that their actions were the result of a premeditated master plan for organizational success. The deception is transparent, and it is another "nail in the coffin" that will eventually put a tombstone on the deceiver's credibility.

Be Discreet

"Children are to be seen and not heard." Parents in my generation used this reminder to dictate a child's behavior in public gatherings. Leaders, due to their public roles, can be tempted to take liberties that are less than discreet. Some may have an obsession to "take center stage" and be the center of attention. Public forums are used to advocate their own agenda or impress others with their profound wisdom or perceived accomplishments. They are opportunistic and have developed the ability to seize the moment. Innovative attempts are disguised in public venues. Public questions or comments are crafted to publicly expose the audience to their proficiency in understanding the subject matter, or program topic. Ironically, they are the only person impressed by their inquiry or comment. The behaviors are designed to be subtle, but the intent is transparent. The wife of a former colleague used sarcasm to kindly rebuke her spouse for his obsession to be the center of attention. She, in jest, often reminded him, "If it is a wedding, you want to be the bride, if it's a funeral you want to be the corpse."

Sensitivity to your personal behavior is critical. We are the last to identify our offensive shortcomings. Insensitivity to the personal views held by others, boisterous conversation, or obnoxious behavior will generate, and even exaggerate, negative interpretations of these behaviors. Remember, leadership is earned, not hyped. An inconsiderate, verbose approach to leadership can leave you with shoestrings between your teeth. The "open mouth, insert foot" syndrome will create unpleasant consequences.

Be Consistent

Have Rules!

Every organization requires structure. Structure is crucial whether it is rigid or relaxed. An organization void of order is given to chaos. Order based on the whim of the leader or the spontaneity required to defuse such folly is not structure, it is confusion. A functional society is founded upon and sustained by order. Order is predicated on absolute perimeters. Meaningful perimeters do not equate to oppressive policies. They simply prevent anarchy and establish guidelines that organizes community. When implemented, all participate equitably.

One can only speculate as to the origin of, what appears to be, society's prevailing tendency to embrace a "Don't tell me what to do mentality." I call it a "No rules society." This mindset subtly found root when disenchantment legalized it. Diverse perceptions of what constitute a citizen's right contributed to an environment that spawned disenchantment. Reactions ranging from rebellious militancy to resentful complacency have found expression in a personal resolve that questions all absolutes. It now seems to be perpetuated as a self-fulfilling prophecy. Historically, it was the private domain of adolescence, but now it invades every facet of our society, and the prognostications are frightening.

Opportunistic leaders who seize the moment and revel in forbidden liberty will reap the consequences of their behavior. A ruleless environment subconsciously inspires subordinates to look for opportunities to rebel against rules and any semblance of authority. It encourages criticism without cause, and spawns suspicion void of supportive reasons. Individuals will be ruled by their suspicions and enslaved by their fears.

Obey the Rules!

"Don't do as I do, do as I say!" Don't send confusing messages. Never demand a standard you do not subscribe to. Leaders that fail to practice what they preach are hypocritical. This behavior is evident in leadership roles of every discipline. Self-centered leaders assume they are "above the law," and are exempt from established rules, policies, and guidelines. "What's good for the goose is good for the gander." Rules, if effectual, are applicable to all. The leader who ignores the authority of organizational policy cannot expect subordinates to obey the rules and subscribe to policy provisions. The leader that rebels against any and all authority is known as a rebel.

The leader that trivializes the importance of structure (rules, regulations, etc.) will create a spirit of anarchy. Your actions can make you the Pied Piper of anarchy. The environment you create can empower subordinates to do their own thing. Biblical warnings portray "doing what is right in one's own eyes" as ill-advised. The book of Judges records the cyclic nature of this folly.

The scandals that besiege corporate America and ravage less prominent organizations can be attributed to those who chose to ignore the rules. Disparity, or selectivity in rule interpretation is unabashed elitism. When an individual places themselves above the rule of order, it blinds them to their inevitable demise. Success, or perceived success can unleash egotistical fantasies. The mad cycle of self-indulgence, self-adulation, and the self-imposed exclusivity of a "society of one," will always lead to an escalation of foolish error. It creates a false sense of infallibility, and this carelessness will claim its victim. Infallibility contradicts logic, escalates error, and enhances the foolishness of risk. The completion of this destructive cycle is evident when episodic rash decisions become more frequent and bizarre. Severe symptoms may be a reflection of either a histrionic or narcissistic personality disorder, or in some cases, a combination of both. There is a difference between personality quirks and personality disorders. A disorder needs treatment.

Send a consistent message. Set the example! Obey the rules! Be certain directives are clear, and that your personal behavior supports both the letter and spirit of established rules. Never allow your actions to annul crucial polices that govern your organization. Your failure to abide by the rules will give subordinates a license to establish their own rules and behave as they choose. The values embraced by your subordinates reflect the values you've demonstrated in your own life. The discipline demonstrated by subordinates will reflect the discipline of the leader.

Be Open

One significant measure of effective leadership is the ability to listen to dissimilar philosophies, opinions, and opposing persuasions without prejudice or judgmental conclusions. This does not mean silence gives consent or endorses error. It simply qualifies the leader to provide intelligent, insightful inspiration, and meaningful leadership. The reciprocal respect you earn will strengthen your leadership role. Individuals are not as averse to differences in opinion as they are not having their opinions valued.

Strongly held opinions are not easily shared by some, while others relish controversy. Regardless of the comfort level of the communicant, your response will either value or devalue the individual. All leaders run the risk of surrounding themselves with colleagues and associates who believe the same thing and subscribe to the same practices. Reality can be altered if differences of opinion are stifled. It is possible a cloister of like minds could uniformly endorse a faulty course of action. The leader's views, even if correct, will deter leadership goals when individuals are devalued.

Be Cautious

Organizational Surprises

Surprises are fun, if for pleasure. "Surprise, surprise, surprise!" became a hilarious trademark of the sitcom character Gomer Pyle. Suffice to say, the "Surprise, surprise, surprise" exercised in a leadership role should be archived. There is a time and place for everything, including surprises, but surprises should be discreetly used. It can be a powerful tool, if used to recognize, reward, or stimulate a constructive work environment. Otherwise, surprises in the workplace are uncomfortable and can be painfully serious. If they become commonplace, they lead to needless suspicion and will have negative consequences. Unexpected changes, or public announcements without prior preparation or notification, create apprehension. On some occasions, surprises are used to disguise inadequate planning by leaders. When leaders are driven by unpredictable, personal leadership deficiencies, the outcomes are predictably unfavorable. The dynamics that build strong organizations make no provision for careless surprises precipitated by incompetent leaders.

You Can Scare a Horse

During the summer in rural Texas, the local Saturday night rodeo is as important as the Friday night football game in the fall. When younger, my brother and I were members of a riding club that participated in some of the opening ceremonies of the local small town rodeos. Each show began with much fanfare, and a riding club would be selected to set pivots in the grand opening ceremonies. Every horse and rider carried a large American or Texas flag. There were no blue ribbons for all the time and energy required, but it was fun, and important to "would be" cowboys. My brother purchased a big beautiful roan mare, and it was suggested she might be ridden in the opening ceremonies for the club's next rodeo engagement. Preparations for the possibility proved to be an unforgettable experience. The animal was bridled, saddled, and mounted for a trial run without a flag. The horse was a pleasure to ride and appeared to respond beautifully for such a routine. The only remaining challenge was to mount the horse with a flag. Precautions were taken to avoid spooking the horse with the colorful flags. Her eyes were shielded as she was mounted, and the large American flag was positioned in the saddle holder. All appeared to have gone well until the covering was removed from her eyes. Her first glimpse of the flag caused her huge body to quiver, and her eyes appeared to dilate. We can only speculate as to what might have happened, had the flag not been quickly discarded. Needless to say, she never set pivots. Surprises can be just as frightening to unsuspecting staff.

Be Yourself

Be careful not to mimic leaders you admire. Regardless of the leadership role, the studious leader will discover a personality, or leadership style, they respect and want to emulate. There is nothing wrong with learning all you can from everyone you can to enhance your proficiency.

The learning process is faulty when the leader loses his or her identity in the process. Be your own person; stake your claim to the ownership of truth principles and release your personality. Personalize the wisdom of others, but don't attempt to be a reproduction of the successes of others. Develop your own leadership style. It may very well be true that your style will become an example for others.

A special word of caution is necessary. If you become a clone of someone else you admire, you will most likely, subconsciously, mimic that person's most undesirable traits. It reminds me of a caricature sketch. The identifiable resemblance is usually the person's most undesired characteristic, and one the individual would prefer not to have.

Be An Example

More Than a Title

What you are and what you do says more about who you are than all you could ever say about yourself. Your life should exemplify a commitment to truth principles. "Lead by example!" Demonstrated character, truth, and commitment create a leader. A leadership role, title, or position will not make you a leader. Individuals in leadership roles should periodically perform candid self-assessments to evaluate the dynamics that identify them as leaders.

"Example is not the main thing in influencing others. It is the only thing."

—Albert Schweitzer

If you are a leader by title only, and you are followed out of necessity, you are only a facsimile of the real thing. Leading by example is a discipline. It is the recognition and acceptance of the fact that the leadership role requires more of you than it does of your followers. Living examples energize subordinates; hype, verbiage, and dishonesty create suspicion, hypocrisy, and superficiality in subordinates.

Earn Your Keep

"Work never hurt anyone." Leaders are not exempt from work. Only "hands on" leadership will stimulate true teamwork. Some leaders delegate their own responsibilities to subordinates, and engage in personal business unrelated to the organization. The spirit of embezzlement is manifest in varying forms. They pull down "big bucks," perform no work, and readily accept credit or recognition for the achievements of others. They relish the title of "boss" and assign subordinates tasks to perform, but they will never achieve the stature of a true leader of people. They will generate resentment and low morale. A "working leader" is an example of what work responsibility is all about.

Your example will set the tone for your program or organization. Your values and example determine the organization's "work ethic." You set precedence. The argument that, "You have paid your dues" turns people off. All feel deserving of the compensation they receive for a job "well done." A leader that fails to carry his or her weight of the workload encourages subordinates to rationalize their own lack of productivity. A "lazy boss" is a detriment to any organization. The expected outcomes of this leadership style will consist of costly innovative shortcuts and establish poor work performance as the "norm."

Be Positive

"Stinking Thinking"

Project a positive image. Positive attitudes and possibility thinking are disciplines. The discipline is a learning process tutored by what you read and those with whom you associate. The natural and immediate response to adversity or disappointments is a negative reaction. No one can truthfully say they are overjoyed by an opportunity created by any adversity in life. One can truthfully say they have learned to react creatively and accept disappointments as challenges for growth. This discipline includes a practice of controlling your environment. All are susceptible to "negative thinking," so it is important to control your exposure to those that habitually demonstrate negative responses to life situations.

It's Contagious!

Exposure to either positive or negative attitudes will have an impact on your life. Both are contagious! Negativism is infectious. Associate with negative thinkers, and you'll catch the disease. It is terminal because it is a disease of the spirit. It will usurp your authority over life's circumstances. All potential for personal, professional, and organizational growth will be stymied. Organizations suffocate under its influence. This is the reason it is important to associate with people who thrive on making good things happen. You'll be captivated by their inspiration.

Attitude is "Your Call!"

Your attitude is the one thing in life you can control. Exercise your authority! Ignore the doughnut holes and enjoy the doughnut. You will either control your attitude, or your attitude will control you. Life isn't a bed of roses, and all of life's stories won't have fairy tale endings. "Don't live under the circumstances, get out from under them," and look for opportunities on which to build your dreams. Your attitude will either be a boost or a burden to you, your career, and your associates. Bad attitudes are a burden to everyone. Positive thinking is a source of encouragement to all.

Quality of life is even an attitude issue. Your attitude not only determines the quality of your own life, it impacts the quality of the lives of others. Be sensitive to the indicators that reflect bad attitudes. Indications of negative obsessions include, "passing the buck," blame, gossip, criticism, and ridicule. Leaders must project a "can do" attitude and then "practice what they preach!" A positive, credible spin is important to counteract routine "downers." Discouraging events are inevitable. Bad things will happen. Effective leaders understand there are two valleys for every mountain, but they also know the most gorgeous scenery is always viewed from the next mountaintop.

Right Perspective

A positive mental attitude is a must, but keep it in perspective. It is a resource of the person's spirit, and has intrinsic value as a support system. It is not an end in itself. Positive thinking doesn't stand alone, but requires energy. Recitation of positive mental attitude clichés, without disciplined directives, is a vain exercise in futility. Positive thinking is not a causative force, it is creative inspiration. Energy and initiative, when applied to creative, innovative thinking, makes positive things happen.

Never sacrifice truth in an attempt to "be positive." Attempts to conceal negative outcomes or events to avoid being negative will stimulate suspicion and distrust. Public disclosure of negative outcomes can be disclosed candidly and publicly in a positive way without forfeiting your credibility or integrity. Attempts to project a positive attitude should never skew the facts or fabricate misrepresentations that mislead.

Be Friendly

Friendliness will change your life. It is so closely linked to courteousness that it could be included in the section to follow. However, it is so important, it deserves special attention. Friendliness changes your environment. Again, you control your own destiny. As a leader, you create the organization's personality. Any corporation, church, organization, or program reflects the personality of its leadership. The friendly leader will lead friendly people. Happy, friendly people are productive people. "A smile is an inexpensive way to improve your looks," and it is also an inexpensive way to improve productivity.

A Lesson From Politicians

Nothing is more crucial to a politician than friendliness. Long-term politicians are long-term because they understand the strength of friendliness. I am not suggesting you have to go so far as to "glad hand," kiss babies, and hug elderly women, but I am saying it is imperative to learn the value of friendliness. A leader's unfriendliness creates a costly distance between the leader and those that have the power to make him, or her, succeed or fail.

The perception a voter has of a politician will always be reflected in the privacy of a voting booth. When the votes are counted, a few friendly actions can be the difference in the outcome of an election. Likewise, the private perceptions of subordinates will find public expression. Impressions are powerful. A positive impression may be evident in unsolicited admiration and enhanced loyalty. A negative impression will echo beyond the silence of the voting booth and will subtly erode leadership persona.

Moodiness is Madness

Part-time friendliness is a disaster. Consistent friendliness is dynamite! The word "moody" should never rear its ugly head in the employment file of a leader. Moodiness will build barriers between you and those you lead. It prohibits meaningful communication and negatively impacts working relationships. The absence of a "mood swing" indicator makes the simplest of tasks difficult. When the unexpected becomes the expected, communication breaks down. Co-workers are unimpressed with rationalizations that moodiness is due to health problems or adverse life circumstances. Every person in your organization has private concerns that are just as crucial, if not more crucial than yours. Every place of business or organization should have a "No Moodiness Allowed" sign on the door. "A man (or woman) who has friends must show himself friendly."

"A stranger is just a friend I have never met."

—Irish Song lyric

Be Sensitive

Check for Leaky Faucets

Home repair, at best, is a nuisance. Plumbing repairs are a nightmare! Words cannot express the exasperation experienced by uncontrolled water spewing from a broken pipe. I am convinced no occupation is more important than plumbers. May their tribe increase! The only thing worse than the panic of a broken pipe is the drip of a leaky faucet. The persistent, methodical drip at 1:30 a.m. on a sleepless night is the most penetrating sound ever experienced by human ear. It may be rhythmic, but there is no rhyme, there is only the drip, drip, drip of sleeplessness.

Repetitious behaviors that annoy are as wearisome as a leaky faucet. They are analogous to monotonous drips. Drips are no respecter of persons. They are inevitable. All have them, at one time or another. Some have them all the time. As a leader, you must keep a regular check on leaky faucets. They may be idiosyncrasies, mannerisms, or repetitious clichés, and stories. A preoccupation with one's personal accomplishments, family members, or personal interests can prove to be extremely annoying. Persistent complaining, boasting, and superficiality are all habits that drip. It would be an impossible task to exhaust the countless possibilities. It is sufficient to say, the effort you make to identify and fix the drips in your life will be time well spent. You'll sleep better and so will your subordinates. Annoying habits have been compared to bad breath and body odor. Usually the offender is the only one that is oblivious to their existence.

Be Decisive

Decisive leadership practices intelligent, long-term, strategic planning. Uncertainty in leadership decision-making is financially and emotionally costly. Good decisions are researched decisions. Effective decisions require extensive planning. Leadership planning must consider benefits, liabilities, barriers, consequences, and potential. The personal interests of all stakeholders must always be paramount in the planning stage.

"Haste makes waste." Decisions should be made based on long-term goals, with constructive short-term implications. Precise decision-making projects a positive image and creates a comfort level for subordinates. Chronic spontaneity and impulsive decisions are, more often than not, emotional reactions, not rational choices. Spontaneous decisions are shortsighted and may be opportunistic. It is possible "quick fix" resolutions will have permanent consequences.

Be Prompt

Act Promptly

"If you snooze, you lose." Procrastination is not a joking matter. It is a waste of irreplaceable time. Time is money! There is little room for levity when you examine the bottom line. It will cost you in lost worker hours and will impede productivity. Chronic procrastination practiced by those in a responsible leadership role will frustrate subordinates. It will negatively impact morale and become a "work place pattern," reflecting persistent breakdowns in operational procedures. Procrastination is a by-product of dysfunctional leadership. It is a testimonial to the leader's perception of his or her fears, inhibitions, and incompetence.

It is a misconception that ignoring a problem changes or solves the problem. You will always have an advantage, if you deal with a problem at its threshold. The continuum from good to bad makes delay a bad option. It is a mistake to believe that delaying a response eases the burden of the decision. Contrarily, it is simpler to address, even difficult tasks, promptly.

Delay, due to complexities, will take a mental toll on the procrastinator and cause undue stress for the one impacted by the decision. A quick elimination of heightened stress and anxiety expedites the corrective process and prevents unhealthy speculations. Procrastination, requiring an unrealistic time frame, can exaggerate, if not create, complimentary problems. Procrastination leads to exacerbation.

Opportunistic Procrastination

Long-range planning schemes that use an avoidance tactic are burdensome. A "wishy-washy" approach to the decision-making process is counter productive and will unleash long-term consequences. Indecision over an extended period of time is unfair to those you rely on to make things happen. The longer one waits, the more difficult the decision and the more laborious the task. Base your decision on truth and act expeditiously.

Leaders that procrastinate are inclined to make decisions as if they were reading a barometer to check barometric pressure. An infusion of peer pressure or political pressure into the decision process prolongs the anguish of difficult decisions and will always result in undesired consequences. Difficult decisions requiring difficult choices are an unpleasant emotional experience. Easy choices are fun! Difficult decisions can either be a challenge or a debilitating fiasco. Procrastination, deceptive innuendoes, inadequate communication, and political maneuvering may all be clever techniques to delay the inevitable, but all delays are costly and have irreparable consequences.

Making difficult decisions and unpopular choices are distinctions of great leaders. "Any fish can swim downstream, only the strong swim upstream." The majority rules in a democratic society, and it should, but the majority can also be wrong. The tenacity to stand alone is a virtue of great leadership. The historical injustices to others and the dehumanization of suppressed ethnic groups in our own nation's history glaringly support this premise. Leaders must be prepared to swim upstream when necessary. Boldness distinguishes the leader and the message. Dr. Martin Luther King's message is still vibrantly clear. His dream has become the dream of succeeding generations. The essence of boldness will be discussed in the next chapter.

Act Responsibly

Likewise, it is important to remember that hasty, unprepared responses can equally have devastating repercussions. Often, time is required to fully assess the consequences of a pronouncement. All have consequences. The consequences may be positive, negative, or a combination thereof. Good choices are knowledgeable decisions that can minimize negative consequences, while achieving positive outcomes. Decision-making skills are learned by experience. Remember, your role as a leader makes you a student of people. If you have done your homework, it will prepare you for prompt intelligent action when the need arises.

Know Your Needs

The zeal to be decisive without adequate research and with limited knowledge is ill advised. All decisions have either a positive or negative impact on those you lead. Your decisions will require the engagement of your followers. Preparation that inspires is more effective than forced participation. You owe subordinates the common courtesy to act on absolutes, not irrational speculations. "Spur of the moment decisions" may cause your horse to buck. I have never forgotten my first pair of spurs and my poorly chosen time to use them. Some horses don't need spurs. Mine didn't! Research the facts and then act. Be certain your zeal is based on sound judgment, not flippant, momentary notions.

"A good horse should be seldom spurred."

—Thomas Fuller

Be Courteous

"Icing on the Cake"

Courtesy is an act or expression of respect and consideration of others. It is the ability to communicate and demonstrate sensitivity to the value of another person. Common courtesies are positive acts taken by a leader to accommodate and convenience subordinates. It accomplishes much.

- It is going the "second mile."
- It is that special effort to recognize those that have been unrecognized. Courtesy finds expression in word and deed.

- It is the art of giving others our undivided attention in conversation.
- It is saying the right thing at the right time to recognize others.
- It is a demeanor and responsiveness that solicits favorable perceptions.
- It is the message, "I value you and care about your concerns."

A courteous leader respects the time and skill of subordinates. Courtesy will never burden subordinates with unrealistic expectations, demeaning instructions, excessive verbiage, or a monopoly of the employee's time, simply to build the leader's own ego.

Make Regular Deposits

Too often, leaders adopt the adage "a little dab will do you." This may be true with a hair-grooming product, but it is insufficient for the work place. Courtesies by leaders build emotional bank accounts. When the organizational or financial aspects of your organization become so stressful or significant that the obsession causes you to overlook common courtesies, you need a priority check. An oversight of the worth of a person and the potential they possess will be the most costly mistake you ever make. If you are too busy to be courteous, you're too busy to lead. The leader's schedule should always include time for a self-inventory of his or her emotional bank account. People wealth is your most valuable asset. Courtesy expends little energy and reaps big dividends. It is the fertile soil for the growth of lifelong, productive relationships. Any behavior that ignores common courtesy will adversely impact the leader.

> "Leadership
> appears to be
> the art of getting others
> to want
> to do something
> you are convinced
> should be done."
> —Vance Packard

CHAPTER 7

PROACTIVE LEADERSHIP

Bold Leadership

There is a chasm between bold leadership and unplanned impulses, or egotistical exploits. Great leadership will require, on occasions, risk-taking boldness without consensus or support. These exploits distinguish great leaders from the mundane. History is replete with leaders who experienced the loneliness of a bold course of action before reaping success. Even great leaders acknowledge these experiences are anomalies rather than routine practices. Adventurous leadership requires preparedness. The leader must internalize the risk, and be prepared to weather the storm.

It should never be a subterfuge for autocratic liberties. The mystique of bold leadership does not justify, endorse, or excuse irresponsible acts that brutalize people or jeopardize an organization. Bold leadership is predicated on extensive planning, consultation, and a premeditated decision-making process. These actions will assess barriers, calculate consequences, and strategize alternatives. Success with bold initiatives will dramatically energize subordinates. It is also true that failure will elicit the same degree of intensity, but with negative results if individuals become disenchanted.

Confidence in the leader's competency is a valuable, intangible asset. The loss of that confidence is costly, and can result in anarchy. It may express itself in overt insubordination, a subtle lackluster performance, or a non-productive free lance spirit.

Planning

The need for planning has been frequently alluded to in earlier chapters. I do not believe its importance could be overly emphasized. Leaders often talk a better game than they play when it comes to organizational planning. "Actions speak louder than words." Poor planning is frequently a glaring fault. Leaders who rationalize it, conceal it, or ignore it, are more deceived by the exercise than those they lead. These leaders are susceptible to their own misrepresentations. When they weave their web of deception, they can expect to become the unwitting quarry. "The grinding wheels of justice may grind exceedingly slow, but they grind exceedingly fine." Nothing is more deafening than a leader's lame excuse for inadequate planning. Individuals that are adversely affected by such carelessness don't need explanations, they need action.

The greater the expenditure of energy, the greater the success rate. Planning will determine the choices you make. Your choices will determine your success. Consider this…the quality of your life, at this present time, is the end result of all the choices you've made in life. The degree of your success will be predicated on the number of discretionary choices you make.

Be sensitive to the fact that the seeds of failure are sown in the planning process. This mindset will require proactive, preventive planning. The right circumstances can result in a full-blossomed failure, if those seeds germinate. Too often, leaders operate under the assumption that only seeds of success are sown in the planning process. The avoidance of hasty planning helps, but it is not a cure all. Prevent the need for pressured or spontaneous planning. These are usually reactionary moves designed to accomplish ulterior motives. If you plant them they will grow. You can reap a bumper crop from the bad seeds you plant!

Activate Your Vision

Plan, then prepare for success. The invigorating leader is driven by a personal vision. Vision necessitates goals. Vision alone is impotent. Vision with only a verbalized goal is meaningless. Goals require defined, methodic action. Constructive action makes visions live. Visions void of planned direction are a disappointment to all. Don't talk a game you can't or won't play. A popular former National League football coach is recognized by his team's claim to fame; they "walked their talk." "If you talk the walk, you have to walk the talk."

Grandiosity Requires Planning

Inspirational challenges have built empires, but grandiose ideas, void of preparation, become the fodder for failure. Hyped, unplanned challenges will play emotional games with the careers and lives of those you lead.

There are at least four explanations for dysfunctional leadership:

1. A lack of planning
2. A lack of principle with ulterior, egocentric motives
3. A lack of knowledge (academically or experientially)
4. A lack of skill (competency) to implement knowledge

Be Proactive

"An ounce of prevention is worth a pound of cure." Preventive action is always a bargain. Don't wait for problems, plan for them. Don't wait for success, plan for it! Success is not accidental. Self-made millionaires planned to be millionaires. Think big and look beyond your plan. Defensive driving courses teach students to have a vision that extends beyond the obvious. Drivers are to look at the big picture and be attentive to any possibility. This instruction focuses on an expectation that dangerous possibilities can, and do occur. Proactive leadership is cautiously progressive.

Work Your Plan

Don't take shortcuts once you have developed a plan. You will short-circuit your power source. Repetitive changes due to poor planning will confuse your most capable leaders and prevent them from utilizing their full potential. Any perception on their part that the leader is operating without defined objectives and planned direction hinders, if not eliminates, the critical emotional dynamic of momentum from the initiative.

Be Versatile

It can be equally devastating when a leader becomes a slave to planning. Some excursions, or restructuring to meet unexpected developments, can prove to be exciting and profitable. There are times when some plans simply do not work. "The best made plans of mice and men…" may have to be tweaked. Life is a learning process, and learning will prompt change. Our society dictates we exercise a readiness to change. The only constant on the "information highway" is change. Today's axiom, "Nothing is as constant as change" requires versatility.

Perception

Several themes are deemed important in this book. I have attempted to note if a conclusion was perception or reality. In some cases, perceptions are a correct interpretation of reality, but all too often it is tainted by circumstances. References through the book embody a spectrum of possibilities from what one may perceive to be true, to what is actually true.

Perception is the pivotal point in all relationships. Perception is everything. It governs relationships, may create anxiety or misrepresent truth, and can birth rumors. Perception is an interpretation of reality. Reality is an interpretation of truth. There is a correlation between perceptions and truth. Truth legitimizes perception and can, if misused, strengthen a misperception. Partial or embryonic truth has the potential to provide credence, even to error.

Truth doesn't change, but it can be misunderstood, misinterpreted, or misused. When the power of perception is underestimated, the consequences are incalculable. The phenomenon emphasizes the need to respect and value perceptions. Remember, perceptions are real to the perceiver. The leader who barters with misperceptions will "pay the piper."

Fear

A concise definition of the word "fear" suggests immediate and long-range negative implications. Fear is a general term that implies anxiety and loss of courage. Fear can be all encompassing. It creates unnecessary apprehensions and hinders sound judgment. One must be sensitive to fearful circumstances and the need for preventive planning, but should never be controlled by them. Adverse consequences, potential difficulties, personality clashes, and perceived barriers are inevitable. Planning predicated on a realistic observation of the broad picture gives the leader confidence and diminishes fear.

Fear of the unseen and unknown is greater than fear of the seen and known. Nothing is more powerful in the human experience than imagination. Imagination has boundless energy and an unlimited potential for either good or evil. When we allow our imaginations to run amuck because of fear, we create impossibilities and impossibility thinking.

Contributing Factors

A word of caution is appropriate regarding the impact that timing, physical health, and the emotional state of mind will have on the planning process. All can contribute to fear if the leader is incapable of healthy introspection. Perceptions can be easily influenced and fears more aptly generated when the leader is physically tired and emotionally exhausted. Appropriate rest will cause some problems to dissipate overnight. The next morning, one may question the fears experienced hours earlier. Don't overlook the fact that problematic issues always impact our emotions.

Miserably Safe

Historically, "fear," when exercised in a leadership role, has resulted in unpleasant, if not tragic, consequences. A leader that routinely allows fear to affect decision-making destroys his or her personal potential. It saps any experience or project of its delight and joy. I have always been fascinated by "the rest of the story," or the untold facts of a story. The historical account of the Jewish Passover has long intrigued me. You probably know the story.

Jehovah proclaimed to Moses he would send a "Death Angel" to pass through Egypt to destroy the firstborn of Egypt. This extreme measure was to change Pharoah's mind and liberate the Israelites. Jehovah gave special instructions to the Israelites to protect them from this display of divine judgment.

The Israelites were to take the blood of a sacrificed lamb and smear the blood on the doorposts of their habitations to ensure the safety of their first born male child. If the Israelites were obedient to this command, the child's safety was affirmed. At midnight, the Death Angel, when passing over Egypt, would pass over any residence that had the blood applied to the doorposts.

Please permit me to speculate. If these fathers and mothers were normal, and they were, can you imagine the anxiety some may have experienced? Their recorded conduct after their liberation from Egypt would suggest that most likely all were impacted by fear. I have wondered how many times they might have returned to re-examine the application of blood on the door, or rehearsed in their minds the process they used to select a lamb. After all, this meant life or death. I have wondered how these fears were expressed. What fears were conjured up by imaginations out of control? "Did I do it right?" "Does this apply to me and my household, or will we be an exception?" "Can this really be true?" The possibilities are limitless. Don't think for a moment there were no apprehensions over this event.

Here is the point of my story. Their safety was ensured by their obedience. If they were obedient, they were safe, regardless of their fears. If they were fearful and anxious, they simply did not experience the relief and joy of their promised safety. If these assumptions are correct, they were "miserably safe." Fear can, and will, negatively impact those life experiences that should be the most meaningful. Leadership should be a positive experience, not a fearful encounter. Fear can rob a leader of the joy and pleasure of success. It can hold you hostage to unfulfilled dreams. It has been suggested, you are most vulnerable to fear and failure immediately following your greatest achievements. "You can't enjoy today when you are preoccupied with fears of tomorrow."

When controlled by fear, you:
1. Never reach your potential.
2. Forfeit your contentment.
3. Surrender your happiness.
4. Distort reality.
5. Lose the excitement of achievement.

To complete this section on fear, it is imperative to look at the power, intervention, and prevention of it. Human nature is addicted to fearful tendencies. Advertisers and marketing schemes capitalize on it. This gives special impetus to the demeanor, words, actions, mannerisms, and plans of the leader. Fear affects every person and every aspect of life. It is spawned by the uncertainties of the unknown. This is true whether it is public speaking, job interviewing, pertaining to our health, or a catastrophic event. Its power deserves attention and caution.

The attentive leader will take immediate action to counteract its crippling potential. Your ability to allay the fears of subordinates is based on the confidence you have in your vision and the plans you have made. This intervention is strengthened by the preventive measures you have taken to overcome defeating barriers. Our greatest moments of strength are severely tested by fear. When fears do develop, and they will, it is a mind thing, and intervention requires you to control your thought process. If you falter, your followers will know it and respond accordingly. Keep your focus on the objective, be resolute, and inspire those you lead. Your demeanor and strength will make a difference. You only give status to fear when you belabor its potential.

The uncertainty of the outcome is the driving force of fear. Knowledge of the processes in place to diminish the cause of fear is very important and helpful. It will eliminate some of the anxiety, but cannot remove all the unknowns. This being true, it is advisable for the leader to take a twofold approach to the power of fear and the intervention needed. First, the leader must provide knowledge and secondly, be supportive of those coping with the anxiety. Information and empathy are important. These approaches should serve to discipline the leader to be sensitive to the spectrum of fear experienced by subordinates.

Franklin Delano Roosevelt reminded a fearful nation,
"We have nothing to fear, but fear itself."

Friendships

"Too Close for Comfort"

"Familiarity breeds contempt." As a leader you must be a friend to all, but a personal friend to none! You may argue, "That statement is ambiguous!" Let me explain. It is imperative that you genuinely befriend those you lead. Their best interests should be paramount with you. A genuineness that says you care cannot be an act on the stage of life. The individuals you lead are sensitive to authenticity and can discern an act from fact. An affirmed demonstration of genuine concern is your title deed to respect.

A personal friendship relationship with those you lead is a luxury you can't afford. You will have difficulty leading those that do not respect your leadership role. It cannot be ignored that personal friendships develop into conditional relationships. There are expectations that evolve from personal friendships. Personal friends expect special relationships. Special consideration is an integral component of a friendship relationship. The relationship may demand special privileges, reciprocity, or leverage for negligent acts. A close friend may expect personal favors, or exceptions to established rules.

Personal friendship, when interwoven with a leadership role, can impede your judgment as a leader. The accountability and responsibility delegated to you may not be congruent with a friendship relationship. To say, as personal friends, "They will understand," is to be naïve. They may report they understand, but pragmatically, they do not, cannot, and will not understand. If you choose to establish close friendships with those you lead, expect to be placed in uncomfortable, precarious situations.

Moral Support Relationships

Another dimension that breathes life into unhealthy personal friendships with subordinates is "the leader under siege syndrome." In the normal course of events, leadership moments will require unpopular decisions and actions that may stimulate resistance from those you lead. Those that are unsympathetic to leadership decisions, under certain circumstances, will enlist others to their cause or persuasions. The leader may reciprocate under the pressure of the moment by establishing close relationships with those sympathetic to his or her cause. This emotional reaction can lead to unhealthy relationships that breed partialities, either perceived or real. It makes the leader pliant and can prevent good judgment. In the heat of controversy, or when under siege by others, a leader can be tempted to "circle the wagons," develop unhealthy relationship bonds, and share confidential information with these trusted subordinates. Divisive decisions and differences of opinion may inadvertently cause a leader to divulge information that is fodder for gossip.

Support System Needed

This is not to say that you shouldn't develop close friendships. In fact, you should and must. Close friendships will provide you an invaluable support system that enriches your life. Constructive friendships developed beyond the sphere of your leadership role allows you the freedom of an unencumbered support system. An inner strength is gained through close friendships. Personal friendships provide emotional sustenance for those inevitable difficult circumstances. Personal friendships are best developed with peers, not subordinates. The value of this support system is enhanced by the objectivity of its members.

Partiality

Every organization has extremely difficult employees. Reasons will vary. It may be a bad attitude, poor performance, a personality clash or jealousy, but all are a challenge. Your challenges with difficult individuals will require a greater expenditure of time and energy. This is an occupational irritant that will have to be contended with on a routine basis.

Even though there are storms, "There is a silver lining to every cloud." You also have model employees who go above and beyond the call of duty. They perform their duties with zeal and strive for perfection. They are visionaries and constantly pursue professional growth. They have positive attitudes and are cooperative. Often their performance is so exceptional, jealous individuals and slothful performers will falsely label them as "brown nosers."

A comment on jealousy is apropos. It has been suggested that, "jealousy is an admission that someone is better than you." Resentment is the destructive component. Jealous resentment can lead, and has led to, hideous and irrational acts. Jealousy is dangerous because it rationalizes any action that leads to self-gratification.

It is only natural to be impressed with, and rely on, your most capable performers. It is vitally important to reinforce excellent performance and reward the performer, but remember, you are the leader of all. You lead good performers, slow performers, poor performers, and phony performers. You have the awesome task of inspiring all, so revere proficiency and reward the performer. Focus your praise on the performance and the performer will be rewarded. Just be sure your praise, recognition, and reward is equitable. Don't be naïve to the evitable.

Beware the Counterfeit

There are individuals who demonstrate the skill of an actor or actress on stage. They mimic desirable traits, heap public praises on their supervisors, and perform solely for preferential treatment. The astute leader should be able to quickly identify such superficiality.

Not only is the identification of this behavior important, the recognition of subsequent behaviors is critical. The zeal demonstrated for self-serving advancement, when ineffective, can be redirected for destructive purposes. An acknowledgement of the existence of these self-serving individuals is sufficient for this discussion. The scorn of co-workers provides them their appropriate compensation.

Remember Your Critics

Your leadership style and mannerisms are constantly under scrutiny. Your deficiencies, suspected, perceived, and real, will be promptly identified and reported by those unsympathetic to your leadership goals. Unsympathetic individuals will most likely exaggerate their perceptions and misperceptions of your leadership intentions.

Disgruntled or dissatisfied individuals will be super-sensitive to your interactions with other staff persons. Any occasion that suggests or leaves a perception of partiality will be opportunistically seized upon to validate their hostile reports. For this reason, it is imperative that you give no occasion, or create situations, to justify charges of favoritism. Secretive meetings and a pre-occupation with private conversations can contribute to unjustified speculations. A failure to keep all staff fully informed of planning strategies, projects, and goals will enhance the fears and suspicions circulated by discontents.

Your reaction to suspicions or allegations of partiality will either extinguish or ignite the perceptions held by staff. You have to create a climate of equality, trust, and fairness. Consistency is the key. Staff must observe it daily and be convinced it's genuine.

Role Model Pitfalls

As a parent, nothing can be more detrimental to a younger sibling in the family than repeated reminders that the elder sibling performs better or is less trouble for the parent. Use extreme caution with role models. Frequent, public, repeated recognition of the personal accomplishments of a single individual to inspire other staff members may be misconstrued. Others may interpret the references as favoritism, and your best intentions may negatively affect them. Perceived or real, partiality demoralizes subordinates. Self-worth is fragile. Handle it with care. The hurt experienced by others can be demonstrative. Jealousy creates suspicion. When your motives are questionable, you fuel the fire.

It cannot be stressed enough, there is no excuse for partiality. Overt favoritism based on personal preferences, or even dependable work performance, will never be tolerated or understood by subordinates. Precautions should be taken to avoid partiality and prevent any perception of it. If you choose to demonstrate partiality, or allow your actions to be suspect, you can expect constant dissension and conflict.

Loyalty

If loyalty is not earned, it is opportunism. Loyalty is defined as being faithful to a person to whom fidelity is due. Dictators demand "blind loyalty." The tendency to evaluate subordinates on the single issue of loyalty reflects the leader's insecurities and fears. Respect for the position of leadership brings with it certain expectations of ethical loyalty, but it does not imply serfdom. Neither do these expectations extend to unethical practices.

Genuine loyalty does not turn a deaf ear to deceitful actions. Leaders need genuine loyalty, but must understand that any show of allegiance apart from what they earn will have opportunistic overtones. Loyalty as an earned benefit strengthens the support system for the leader. It is certain that all leaders have critics and self appointed opponents. The loyalty of subordinates creates a support system that fortresses the leader's objectivity and counteracts negativism. Don't expect it, unless you earn it.

Advice

Unsolicited Advice

Decision making advice must be good advice! Seek out wisdom, but exercise discernment. It is important that you discreetly use advice. Advice, whether volunteered or solicited, can result in bad choices. Some advice will have a life of its own, creating long-term consequences. Don't overlook indicators that suggest the need for close scrutiny. The fact that some individuals are prone to habitually offer unsolicited advice is a red flag of caution. Most likely these individuals do not have the expertise or knowledge they profess to possess. They provide information on any subject and profess to have extensive experience to support their claims. The information they provide is always couched in personal illustrations, most of which are untrue or exaggerated, to focus attention on themselves. These crude attempts are subconscious admissions of the lack of fulfillment and recognition they have experienced in their own professional lives.

Know-It-All Ignorance

Consultation and advisement is necessary, but the resource must be credible and confidential. Flawed consultation will result in serious judgment errors. Caution is advised when your source has answers to questions that have never been asked and makes a point to impress you, and others, with his or her knowledge base. There is nothing worse than verbose "know-it-all" ignorance. Fabricated knowledge by an individual that knows just enough to make them dangerous will produce irreversible consequences. Usually these individuals have the capability of fantasizing into reality aspirations never realized or achieved. The intensity of the recitation, and the frequency of spiraling exaggerations are the reflections of the remorse they experience over their own failure. Repetition rewrites history for the prevaricator. Ultimately, the woven web of deceit appears to affirm the fallacious reports of the perpetrator. Careless consultation is avoidable.

Personal Baggage Alert!

Advice always has the potential to be contaminated by the advisor's personal baggage. The baggage may be prejudices that were formulated on past failures, fears, disappointments, and/or rationalized mistakes. Objectivity can easily be lost in well-intentioned advice. There are simply too many variables to ignore extreme caution. I will name a few to illustrate my point. An individual's professional history or life story includes circumstances, traditions, varied organizational structures, diverse sizes of organizations, differing cultures, a variety of interactive dynamics, diverse ages of organizations, personal successes and failures, different leadership styles, personalized opinions, personal values, character traits, and an array of leadership philosophies. We, individually, are a by-product of our exposure to, and experience with, any or all of these variables. An individual's reaction to the life experience shapes philosophies, molds leadership styles, and influences the decision-making process. If the decision process is flawed, the advice is flawed.

Personalize Advice

"Every tub sits on its own bottom." This is not to say that you can't learn from, and benefit from, those that have graduated from the "School of Hard Knocks." It is only an urgent reminder that discernment is crucial. Accept advice based on the applicability of the information to your own personal needs or the needs of your organization. Discernment and the application of good advice are only possible after you have gained a thorough knowledge of your own organization's variables. Applicability is the key; discernment is selecting the right lock. Don't overlook the obvious. Even though you can learn from the mistakes and successes of others, you must be aware of the fact you can also learn and practice the mistakes of others. Practices reflecting successes that have little or no applicable resourcefulness are of little value to you or your organization. Every organization is unique, so personalize advice!

Compliments

Give Them!

Everyone enjoys a compliment. Leaders should discreetly and frequently use them to inspire subordinates. Compliments reflect gratitude and acknowledge the worth of employees. They reinforce commitments, work ethics, and loyalty to the organization. Personally, they motivate professional ambitions and are welcomed by the employee. The singular most important component of a compliment is sincerity. We are all uncomfortable with insincere or ritualized compliments that are nothing more than useless gibberish.

Don't Solicit Them!

Don't solicit compliments! If you do, people will resent it. Even subtle attempts to glean compliments are recognized for what they are, a sign of leadership insecurity or egoism. If your performance deserves commendations, you will receive them. Solicitation of coerced exaggerations from others will, in retrospect, likely conclude with resentful reactions on their part. Success speaks loudly, but resentment will speak more loudly.

Don't use the pretense of public recognition for staff to focus the spotlight on your perceived successes. If you do, your ploy will be transparent.

Get Real!

Compliments are given for differing reasons. Well meaning admirers frequently use compliments to gain favor and reciprocal friendship. Opportunistic, "brown nosers" heap praises on persons in leadership roles for personal gain. These individuals can hold a leader, desperate for recognition, hostage. Again, the susceptibility is either a reflection of the leader's insecurity or an "ego trip." In both cases the leader can expect, at some point in time, an unpleasant experience with the "brown noser." The word is in the dictionary and its meaning is, to say the least, demeaning. The definition reads, "The implication that servility is equivalent to kissing the hinder parts of the person from whom advancement is sought." It is slang for the implications of ingratiating oneself to another.

When, as a leader, you can appreciate compliments without taking them too seriously, it is your first "baby step" to leadership maturity. Many compliments are genuinely sincere, but most are mere expressions of kindness or gratitude. Every young minister has had some sweet little lady tell him that he preaches just like Dr. Billy Graham. The problem is, some believe it! Any and all compliments deserve appreciative recognition by the recipient.

Selfishness

A "what's in it for me" mindset causes individuals to focus on who they are, and what they hope to become. The inclination, if habitual, can become an obsession. Obsession leads to an illogical thought process. Paradoxically, individuals subscribing to selfishness may experience resentment toward others who practice it. Personal guilt is supersensitive and often seeks to express itself. It finds expression in judgmental and caustic criticism. This behavior proclaims the hypocrisy of guilt imposed actions.

The generosity or selfishness of a leader is best measured by his or her attitude regarding financial compensation for subordinates. Leaders that pursue excessive compensation for their own services, but are stingy with subordinates are selfish. It undermines their credibility and will subsequently impact their ability to lead. No degree of demonstrated proficiency justifies inequitable compensation practices. It is certain that an obsession for personal gain never takes into consideration one's own leadership deficiencies or a demonstrated ineptness to lead. Professed care for staff members and frequent adulation, without appropriate compensation, will be perceived as cheap to a dedicated employee. The very connotation of the word "cheap" should be motivation enough to avoid the stigma. Self-centeredness reeks with the stench of a putrefaction process that originates in the character of an individual. Stinginess can't disguise itself as frugalness. There is a distinct difference between the two.

Change

The Paradox of Change

Resistance to change is as real as the inevitability of change. Denial of change creates a utopian fantasy world that never has, nor ever will exist. My generation may be tempted to peer into the past through rose-colored glasses and visualize what never was. The life experience is one of change. My generation witnessed more significant change than any that preceded it. The stability of an agricultural society, and even that of an industrial society yielded predictability, but both eras were fraught with change. We have traveled from horse and buggy to a space shuttle with breathtaking speed. The world is now our community, and we are compelled to make change our companion. We change, families change, and our vocations change making change the only constant in life. The frequency of change has not diminished either the dislike or fear we experience when encountering it. The dynamic of change and the human response to it is predictable. This predictability should sensitize the delicacy with which we approach change and the care we administer during change.

A Curve or a Dead End?

I am intrigued by a message on a motivational poster and coffee cup that reads, "A bend in the road is not the end of the road...unless you fail to make the turn." Change, too frequently, is the end of the road for our dreams, aspirations, and goals. Roads do curve, have potholes, and are often cluttered with debris. All are hazardous to the traveler's safety and comfort, but all are a part of the trip. All require spontaneity. When emergencies necessitate a reaction, planning is not an option. Only the road once traveled provides an opportunity for a degree of planning. Most roads in life have not been traversed. Perhaps the moral of such an analogy is, "accepting change as your plan is better than trusting experience for a plan." Life's junkyards are filled with the wreckage of those who failed to negotiate the curves.

Five key components are critical to implement effective and harmonious organizational changes:

1. Consensus of Staff: Change is exciting and crucial to longevity. Nothing stagnates more than tradition without purpose. Organizations must change to remain competitive and relevant. Research has documented a correlation between adaptability to change and long life. This is certainly true with organizations. Expect fear! Change creates fear and must be delicately handled. Carelessness with change exacerbates anxiety due to the unpleasantry of leaving a comfort zone. Moving from the known to the unknown can be traumatic. People do not like change and, more often than not, will resist it. The leader's ability to stimulate change will be determined by his or her ability to recognize the need for it. Once people are convinced of a need, they will become co-partners in its pursuit. Genuine change is achieved by consensus, not coercion or command.

2. Plan Ahead: Change should be the end result of a well thought out plan, including contingencies for barriers, liabilities, objections, costs, and benefits. Key individuals, or stakeholders, should be enlisted in the planning process. The opportunity to strategize and participate creates ownership. Ownership stimulates endorsement and encourages participation. Change breathes new life into dead carcasses. All organizations can benefit from constructive change. Change is more than necessary; it is required if an organization is to be vibrant and effective. Change is being futuristic.

3. Establish Need: As important as they are, changes must be relevant and constructive. "Change for the sake of change," creates confusion and chaos. "If it ain't broke, don't fix it." The driving force for change must be necessity. Changes by leadership are motivated by a full gamut of possibilities. Leaders have attempted to establish their

own credibility or impress their peers by inflicting needless change on organizations. Egocentric embellishments, designed to rewrite the history of an organization, have been used to obscure the notable achievements of predecessors. The novice has been known to use frequent, repetitive changes to conceal a lack of knowledge. Motivations for change, of this nature, are a reflection of the leader's immaturity, egocentricity, and lack of direction.

4. Value Past Accomplishments: Change must respect the successes of an organization. Failure to acknowledge historical successes, or an attempt to ignore them, will create resentment by those responsible for those successes. People are proud of past accomplishments, and a wise leader will build on that fact. Their expertise can prove to be an invaluable resource for your own success. A belief, or actions indicating a belief that nothing is worthy of preservation will result in crippling isolation for the leader. The perception of elitism will distance you from those that you must rely on for your success. An understanding of the organization's "sacred cows" based on a thorough comprehension of existing dynamics is a required pre-requisite to change. When handled discreetly, "Sacred cows make the best hamburger." The older an organization is, the greater the need for extensive research. The greater the success of an organization, the greater the need will be to exercise cautious respect for historical accomplishments. Longevity in any organization is "proof positive" that functional processes have been historically utilized and many still exist. Don't rewrite history to justify meaningless change. Reckless changes "throw the baby out with the bath water."

   "You shouldn't take a fence down until you know the reason it was put up."

                                                    —G.K Chesterton

5. Be Consistent: Consistency is a virtue; inconsistency is a vice. To some, inconsistency is a lifestyle. It becomes the only constant in life. Inconsistency is inconsiderate, selfish, and rude. Inconsistency speaks volumes. It is a leadership deficiency. Habitually, inconsistent leadership cloaks inadequacy as change. The merits of healthy change are discredited by irresponsible change.

It has been said, "Lack of planning on your part doesn't necessarily create an emergency on my part." The truth is, inconsistent change does and will create an "emergency room" environment. Triage will rule the day, and the casualty list will loom large. Irresponsible change is the culprit of inconsistency. Insult is added to injury when the conduct is excused or depicted as a management strategy. The vice is evidentiary. Its outcomes convict the practitioner of incompetence, ill-preparedness, skill deficits, and other debilitating practices. When defining crime as any serious wrongdoing, it becomes a crime against subordinates. Inconsistency is a blatant violation of trust. It erodes confidence in the leader's ability to lead. Personal or organizational inconsistencies create havoc by sowing seeds of confusion, resentment, and dissent. A credible singular change can be a taxing experience without the burden of inconsistency. So caution is commendable. Inconsistent practices, like inconsistent behaviors require attention and intervention.

History can be, and perhaps is, our most prolific resource on change.

> "We trained hard, but it seemed that every time we were beginning to form up into teams we were reorganized. I was to learn later in life that we tend to meet any new situation by reorganizing, and what a wonderful method it can be for creating the illusion of progress while actually producing confusion, inefficiency, and demoralization."
>
> —Petronius Arbiter, 210 B.C.

Integrity

"Practice What You Preach"

Integrity is an earned honor. It is not by osmosis or heredity. Character is the moral nature of a person that defines reputation and conduct. Integrity is the firm adherence to a moral code of honesty. Integrity and character are inseparable. It is who we are, not what we say we are. Publicly talking about it does not make it experiential. In fact, talk without substantive evidence is nothing more than fabrication.

Respect is a fringe benefit of integrity, and integrity is the by-product of practiced truth.

It expands our horizons and creates opportunities. It equips us, experientially, to see the servant's towel and the opportunities it offers. The importance we place on being what we ought to be will allow us to do what we ought to do. Doing without being will never see the small opportunities. Greatness is best depicted on the canvas of insignificance.

Leadership that is not truth centered will be short lived. There are no leadership roles for falsehoods, misrepresentations, and half-truths. As discussed earlier, half-truths are more dangerous than an absolute lie because the power of a single embryo of truth gives credibility to a lie. The leader who resorts to "half-truth leadership" is more dangerous because the deception is more effective. Practice truth. Be an advocate of truth.

> "Whatever is only almost true is quite false and among the most dangerous of errors, because being so near truth, it is the most likely to lead astray."
>
> —Henry Ward Beecher

Truth is Still the Issue!

Truthfulness is a character issue. Absolute truth is established on the premise of absolutes. Its origin is divine. The failure to accept absolutes, or the existence of the divine, eliminates right and wrong. It allows the leader the exclusivity of interpreting and exercising truth at the leader's discretion. This is an intrusion by the leader into the divine. The leader becomes the author of truth. His or her perceptions, desires, and opinions eliminate any system of checks and balances and will, eventually, wreak havoc in any organization. The practice of such a philosophy is the germinated seed from which cults are born. A lie disguised by misleading terms, innuendos, or non-verbal communication is a breach of a divine principle. Deceptive practices have the potential to unleash unthinkable hostilities. There is no greater insult or hurt to be experienced by an individual than the realization they have been deceived by a lie. It victimizes and leaves one feeling violated. Character is evidenced in the leader's practice of truth, and commitment to it, regardless of the circumstances. Truth sometimes hurts, but it is always therapeutically healthy. It is healthy for both the practitioner and the recipient. If the truth is hurtful, it will require skill, tact, concern, and empathy from a competent leader to make it a therapeutic experience. Truth is not brash or abrasive; it is candid and considerate.

Mediocrity

Don't Stagnate!

"Anything worth doing is worth doing right." Mediocrity is of moderate or low quality, value, ability, or performance. Some individuals are interested in drawing breath and salary. They are a burden to the organization and their peers. Likewise, there are leaders who achieve a degree of success, and then find a comfort level that requires little challenge and no incentive. On a continuum from worst to best, they are content to be average. On a scale from one to ten, that's a five. Organizations either grow or self-destruct. Leadership objectives designed to only achieve the acceptable, or the norm, are unacceptable. The norm stagnates. Stagnation breeds lethargy, rationalization, and criticism. Contentment with this level of performance leads to self-fulfilled prophecies of doom and gloom. As illustrated on the following chart, the leader that is content to be just "average" must determine which of two categories they find more honorable. Is it better to be the best of the worst or the worst of the best?

BEST

(WORST OF THE BEST)

---------------- AVERAGE ----------------

(BEST OF THE WORST)

WORST

James Bowie, School Superintendent, Goldthwaite, Texas

"Only mediocrities rise to the top in a system that won't tolerate wave making."

—Laurence J. Peter

"Don't be a Slave to the Past"

Successful organizations, or individuals, did not become successful by being content to be just "average." Success requires a commitment to excellence, and excellence requires due diligence. If an organization, or an individual, reaches a state of mediocrity, growth ceases. When growth ceases, the consequences are disastrous. Their subsistence is predicated on the past. Whether real or perceived, past failures, or successes, have the potential to dictate the present as well as the future. Past failures can make one susceptible to fulfilled prophecies of the same in the future. Past successes can lead to traditions void of futuristic value. Every successful organization, or leader, must constantly be on guard to avoid and prevent lethargic philosophies and practices. "You can't rest on your laurels." Historical acclaims to fame will not suffice for future accolades. The failure to recognize and value the cost of success will be costly.

Confidentiality

A Sacred Trust

Practice confidentiality! Sensitive information handled carelessly will create frightening consequences. Exercise extreme caution when sharing information with associates or subordinates. If there is no consent for release and no "need to know," the sharing of confidential information is gossip. Confidential information is a trust, and you, by nature of your possession, become the trustee. I would even consider it a sacred trust. Stewardship defines your responsibility. Greater care should always be given the property of others by a steward. The unapproved release of confidential information, by accident, or on purpose, is inexcusable. Your action allows others the opportunity to capitalize on the defenselessness of betrayed trust. Confidentiality as a sacred trust requires self-control. The meaning of the root word for self-control in the Greek language is, "to take hold of." Leaders must keep a firm grip on confidential information.

Confidentiality is fragile. It requires proper care and storage. The consequence of betrayed trust is a loss of trust, a loss of respect, and permanent damage to the relationship. Once betrayed, forgiveness for the act may be possible, but trust will be irretrievable. The quality of the relationship will never be the same. Future associations and relationships will retain the stigma and unpleasant memory of betrayed confidentiality. Hurt finds expression, and a by-product of the hurt can be information shared with others regarding the betrayal. Trust is the leader's most valued asset. Don't foolishly sacrifice it!

Leaders must exercise extreme caution because of the sheer volume of information they are exposed to, have access to, or receive. Good intentions, accidental remarks, or careless oversights, without malice, are just as hurtful as a premeditated betrayal of confidentiality. A safe rule to remember is, "There can be no confidants when it comes to the confidentiality of others."

Humor

It's Powerful!

Keep a good sense of humor. Never underestimate the power of humor. It has been used by the entertainment industry to do everything from market laxatives, to debase the moral values of our nation. Appropriately used humor can diffuse tense situations and it always offers a refreshing interlude. Under no circumstances, in a leadership role, should humor ever be used at the expense of others. People will respond when you laugh with them, but they will resent it if you laugh at them. Humor, at your own expense, is acceptable, if done tastefully. You can always say more with a smile than you can with a frown. "A smile greatly increases face value." It has been suggested, "Laugh, and the whole world will laugh with you, cry, and you cry alone."

Proverbs 17:22
> "A merry heart doeth good like a medicine: but a broken
> spirit drieth up the bones."

—King James Version

It's Personal!

Humor and kindness will humanize an organization. Both generate a relaxed, caring atmosphere that will contribute to the quality of life in the work environment. Individuals who enjoy their environment are more responsive, productive, tolerable, and flexible to the everyday demands or frustrations of the work place. Leaders should be sensitive to every opportunity to see the humor in any situation, difficult or otherwise. Seize the moment to make someone's life more pleasant.

It's Not Planned!

Humor is not something you plan. If you do, it is artificial, it loses its impact, and it is counterproductive. Life is filled with humor, but it requires sensitivity to recognize it. Humor must be natural. Spontaneity, seasoned with humor, can invigorate life with new perspectives. Nothing is more offensive than a façade or an attempt to create humor for humor's sake. Superficiality reeks with hypocrisy and engenders the scorn of those subjected to it. Public speakers know well the value of genuine humor to relax an audience. They likewise know the horror of failed humor. The dynamic of energizing humor is effective in any setting.

Planned humor in your role as a public speaker is apropos, but even then it should be natural, and an expression of your personality. Joke telling is not for everyone. Some have an unusual ability to recall every joke they have ever heard. Usually these individuals are natural joke tellers. Those of us that have to be careful with jokes can inflict on our listeners an awkward moment, while personally enduring the embarrassment of "egg on our face." As a leader, you can use jokes, as long as they flow naturally, are appropriate, and not "off-color," or ill-intended. Ungifted joke tellers can more effectively access humor by capitalizing on events or circumstances that provide the opportunity for levity. It is important to be sensitive to humor and to value it as a personal enrichment resource.

Vision

It is prudent to expand our discussion on vision in this separate section due to its importance. Biblical admonition regarding the importance of a vision uses forceful language. "Without a vision, the people will perish." Vision has been defined as the power of perceiving that which is not actually present to the eye, whether by supernatural thought, imagination, or clear thinking. A vision inspires, gives purpose for living, and provides an opportunity for fulfillment. Inspire before you attempt implementation!

Loose your Imagination!

"Can't never could do anything." Expect failure and you'll get failure. Defeatism scorns success. Captives of failure create their own prisons. You must envision success before you realize it. If you can't envision success, you wouldn't be able to recognize it if you accidentally achieved it. A leader must be a visionary. Permit your imagination to dream impossible dreams. The only limitation you have is the choice you make to limit your own imagination. All that exists, good or bad, is the result of someone's imagination. Imagine the unimaginable, and you will do the unthinkable. Great leaders have the ability to stimulate an imagination that leads to creativity. True visionary leadership is motivated by an imagination that models creativity.

"Imagination is more important than knowledge."
—Albert Einstein, American physicist

Be Practical

Expect to be misunderstood and criticized, but don't generate criticism. The difference between visionary leadership and grandiosity is marginal. Merriam Webster's Collegiate Dictionary defines the difference.

Grandiosity is characterized by affectation of grandeur, or splendor, or by absurd exaggeration. It is the act of taking on or displaying an attitude or mode of behavior not natural to oneself or not genuinely felt. A visionary is one whose ideas or projects are impractical and unreal, but they are not encumbered with hypocrisy.

Embrace visionary goals, but avoid the persona of either absurd exaggerations or impractical objectives. Absurdities are only grand to the owner. Visionary inspiration has the potential to be community property.

Don't lose sight of reality in the process. You can build "air castles" on non-existent foundations. Leadership vision requires attention to detail and reality. Build your castles, but be sure you have a foundation with no cracks that will destroy your dream. Anchor your foundation on proven leadership principles.

Be prepared to turn loose. Some visionary goals will not be realized. There is a difference between a commitment to a vision and an obsession with it. If it doesn't work, don't obsess over it, move on. A vision energizes, it doesn't stigmatize. There is a myriad of reasons why some visionary goals never happen. The Dakota Indians passed tribal wisdom from generation to generation that could apply to a leader who refuses to accept the fact that their visionary goal will not happen. It advised, "When you find that you are riding a dead horse, the best strategy is to dismount." The moral of the story is clear: if the horse dies, bury it, don't ride it. Obsessing can lead to desperate measures, and desperate measures will have you beating a dead horse.

Burnout

The Quest for Success

Technology's utopian promise of more leisure time and less stress did not materialize. Technology and prosperity have generated a hedonistic society fueled by unlimited opportunities and unrealistic demands. An insatiable appetite for success, acclaim, and wealth, now make young professionals old before their prime. Whether the organization is for profit, or a not-for-profit charitable entity, the demands are the same. Leaders, whether they are an executive officer, director, politician, priest, pastor, or rabbi, must deal with it from two perspectives; their own, and those they lead.

An obsession with success is the successful leader's Achilles' heel. Successful CEOs are tempted to endlessly pursue the elusive dream of success. Pastoral leaders are not immune. Some have frequently relocated and proclaimed the move to be "God's will," when in truth, they were either pursuing their perception of success, or they only needed a sabbatical, not a move. Relocation gives a "six month honeymoon" before the quest and the subsequent burnout is recycled.

Terrible Consequences!

"Burn-out" means worn out or exhausted. "Don't burn the candle at both ends" is a word of caution that individuals should not indulge in prolonged stress, overwork, or intense activity that would result in fatigue, frustration, and apathy. Individuals experiencing burn-out demonstrate a variety of symptoms ranging from denial, to depression, to emotional outbursts. Ill-timed job relocations, irrational behaviors of seclusion, or escapism may be indicators of disguised burn-out. In some cases, it is recognized for what it is and is, properly dealt with. However, in too many situations, the outcomes are at least unpleasant, if not self-destructive. The individual that chooses to deny it will self-destruct. Bizarre behaviors, bad health, domestic difficulties, and chemical or alcohol dependency are only the tip of the iceberg. If the truth were known, the consequences of severe burnout would most likely be startling. Not to overly dramatize the issue, but to emphasize its importance, I would remind the leader that contorted perceptions of success have left a trail of suicides, homicides, domestic violence, child abuse, and a variety of other sordid behaviors.

An Accepted Fact of Life

Time lines are crucial. Attention to task can be a stressor, and due diligence is a must, but remember this, "the world was not created in one day." Urgency is required in the leadership role, but common sense should prevail. Burnout has become an accepted fact of life. Failures to manage time, value people, plan properly, effectively delegate, and exercise realistic expectations, are principle ingredients in the recipe for burnout.

A Bad Choice

Burnout is a lifestyle choice. If you choose, you can abbreviate your career and experience the adverse circumstances of that bad choice. I remind you again, the quality of your life, at this present time, is the sum total of life's choices to date. The stakes are high. Personal relations, marriage, family, and your health are all at risk. Some things are irreplaceable, and the sacrifice is not worth it. The Lord created a Sabbath for rest. He made the earth in six days and then rested. The fact that individuals need rest is a divine principle. When a divine principle is violated, the consequences are intrinsic. "All work and no play makes Jack a dull boy or Jill a dull girl."

Teamwork

Merriam Webster's dictionary states that a team is committed to teamwork rather than individual achievement. It is comprised of several associates or members individually doing their part, but all subordinating personal prominence to the efficiency of the whole. Major corporations learned quickly the value of self-directed work teams. The synergy generated from group dynamics and collective brainstorming revolutionized their organizations.

Organizations, whether non-profit or for-profit, historically relied on committees to expedite projects and stimulate creativity. The results, at best, have been limited and chronically divisive. Too often, committees have either not been empowered or have become socialized entities that equate to a status symbol. Many consist of structure without results. Output without outcomes is busy work. Two extremes are usually represented; one is a committee that attempts to control everything, the other is a committee in name only.

> "What is a committee? A group of the unwilling, picked from the unfit, to do the unnecessary."
> —Richard Harkness

C. Gene Wilkes in his book entitled, *Jesus on Leadership*, made a worthy distinction between committees and teams; "Committees control, but teams empower." Committees maintain the status quo, while teams energize new opportunities for growth. Committees usually are not empowered to implement changes; they are only empowered to make recommendations. The "tongue in cheek" expression that "A camel is a horse created by a committee" captures the frustration often experienced when assessing committee outcomes. Teams most often are more effective when empowered to pursue and facilitate organizational growth.

Long-term committee positions are an additional pitfall of committee structures. They engender personal control issues, where as short-term team initiatives eliminate these traditions of control.

> "Meetings are indispensable when you don't want to do anything."
> —John Kenneth Galbraith

The dynamics of empowered teams through shared leadership can be visually understood in the " 'G' is for Goose analogy."

"G" is for Geese

Geese are interesting creatures. They truly know how to create an effective and efficiently empowered team. Their natural ability to model "shared leadership" within a team is a phenomenon that deserves further scrutiny by human beings. Let's consider these observations that wildlife experts have made about geese. Notice how the actions of the geese in flight provide a positive model for empowered teams.

Example #1:

Geese fly in a "V" formation. Flying in this pattern enables them to migrate 60 to 70 percent farther than if each bird flew unaccompanied. As each goose flaps its wings, it creates less wind resistance for the bird following it in the "V" formation.

Insight #1:

Team is an acronym for "Together Everyone Achieves More." Like the geese, people can truly live this philosophy too. Indeed, sharing a common direction, and supporting one another can enable the team to achieve great things.

Example #2:

Obviously, a V-shaped formation requires that there be a lead goose where the two lines of geese come together. The lead goose is not always the same bird. Most of the geese take a turn on the point of lead position. When the lead goose begins to tire, it moves back to a regular support position along one of the lines of the "V." Another goose then rotates into the point position, and takes its turn fighting into the wind and leading the flock from the point position.

Insight #2:

It pays to rotate leadership. By rotating leadership, more than one individual on the team gets a chance to grow and expand his or her skill base. Furthermore, team members don't have to depend on one person always being the leader.

Example #3:

Some geese stay inside the "V" structure. These geese are too old or too weak to take their turn at the front of the "V" formation, or in a support position along either line of the "V" formation.

Insight #3:

We have to understand people's strengths and weaknesses within a team framework. We must look for each person to contribute to the best of his or her ability.

Example #4:

Geese honk as they fly. However, observers of geese tell us that the lead goose (the one on the point) never honks. Wildlife observers theorize that the geese behind the leader honk praise, encouragement, and support to the lead goose.

Insight #4:

Recognition, praise, and encouragement are the glue that holds and bonds teams together.

Example #5:

Invariably, a goose may feel a need to leave the formation and go down to the ground. Perhaps the goose feels ill, has been wounded, or needs a drink of water. When this happens, two other geese leave the formation and escort this goose to the ground. They go with this bird in order to protect and support it. These escort geese will stay with the goose until it dies. If it does not die, the escort geese help the goose return to the formation, or they find another formation of geese to join.

Insight #5:

When times are tough, team members need to support one another. Teamwork requires commitment through the "rough patches," as well as the good times.

Example #6:

There are always a few geese (or perhaps one goose) that are flying by themselves a few yards away from the "V" formation. Experts believe that these geese are scouting for a better wind current or a more productive way for the flock to travel.

Insight #6:

Teams must adhere to the notion that there is always a way to work smarter rather than work harder. The notion of constant improvement through teamwork is the essence of creating a quality organization.

(Author Unknown)

Team initiatives must be determined by need, not convenience, or ulterior motives. Don't succumb to the temptation to opportunistically substitute a team approach for indecisive leadership. If you do, you will sacrifice leadership on the altar of complacency.

Temper

Negative Consequences

The word's meanings proffer ambiguity. One can temper a bad situation or one's bad temper can create the situation. Temper, in a negative connotation, is a state of feeling, or frame of mind at a particular time, usually dominated by a single emotion. It is defined as a heat of emotion or proneness to anger. It is a lack of self-control. All are vulnerable to anger and have experienced moments that demonstrated a lack of self-control. A bad temper is hostility out of control.

Chronically practiced, it will cost a leader his or her respect, and will stifle the professional growth of subordinates. If one is incapable of self-discipline, he or she is incapable of exercising constructive discipline when and where it is required. The behavior is scorned by subordinates and engenders private resentment that will seek public expression.

A Growth Opportunity

Bad tempers are costly, financially and emotionally. Responsible leaders should be concerned over both negative outcomes. Self-control is a required credential to make good hiring choices and properly train those that are hired. The ability to control one's own temper is imperative. It models appropriate behavior to assist subordinates that may be struggling with destructive tempers.

Bad temper is a learned bad habit. It is opportunistically used and reinforced by the kindness of those who choose to acquiesce to avoid unpleasant encounters. Children learn quickly that temper tantrums can be the shortest route to obtaining what they otherwise could not have. Only maturity with growth alters the habit. It is the squeaky wheel syndrome. "The squeaky wheel gets the grease."

Operation Rescue

Competent individuals in the work place who "fit and quit" should be considered a challenge to creative leaders who recognize the behavior as a growth opportunity. This behavior pattern should be confronted quickly because it is a precedent setting behavior. Without intervention, the reaction becomes an individual's response to all adversities in life. Repetition becomes a habit. The timely response may rescue a productive worker from a self-destructive, life-long pattern, and prevent additional retraining costs for your organization.

Chronic reactionary patterns will destroy the potential of a productive worker. The leader should prevent, if possible, the impoverishment of unproductive spontaneity. When these "emotionally charged" individuals are redirected, they have the potential to make good things happen. If redirection is not possible, their zeal, ability, and potential will set in motion an endless cycle of employment change.

Constructive Anger

Anger is an emotion. Constructive anger can be a positive force to bring change. The Bible admonishes individuals to "be angry and sin not." Christ demonstrated anger toward the money-changers in the Temple. He turned over tables to make a point. It is an intense emotional state induced by displeasure. The inability to be emotionally motivated will make an individual prone to mediocrity. If a cause or principle is worthy, it deserves emotional energy. "If you can't stand for something, you will fall for anything." Intense emotion is often required to change difficult situations and dysfunctional systems. Coaches are emotional because they are competitive. They motivate by emotion and use it to gain an edge on their opponents. Good athletic coaches emotionally seize the moment to gain "momentum." Controlled constructive anger, without malice, can be a forceful motivation. Its use should be an exception and not the rule. Anger harbored will become bitterness. When anger is expressed, get over it, and do it quickly!

Control Your Anger

"Who is mighty? One who can control their emotions and make of an enemy, a friend."

—The Talmud

We are emotional beings, so never fear your emotions. Don't be enslaved, or embarrassed by them. You should fear either a lack of emotional commitment, or an emotion out of control. Avoid either extreme! A chronic public display of anger is a testimony one has lost the ability to control their emotions. This loss will equate to a loss of respect by peers and subordinates.

A select group of individuals are simply angry, miserable people. Angry people rationalize their anger and justify their behaviors. Rationalization may be, based on life's circumstances, a resentment that they had to "pay their dues," or may even be egotistically driven by the perception that subordinates require autocratic leadership. Uncontrolled anger is counter-productive. Malicious anger is dangerous.

"No one else 'makes us angry.' We make ourselves angry when we surrender control of our attitude. What someone else may have done is irrelevant. We choose, not they. They merely put our attitude to a test. If we select a volatile attitude by becoming hostile, angry, jealous, or suspicious, then we have failed the test. If we condemn ourselves by believing that we are unworthy, then again, we have failed the test."

—Jim Rohn

Arrogance

"Big Shots"

"Whatever goes around comes around." Arrogance is self-destructive. Don't let your position "go to your head." Nothing is resented more than individuals who feel themselves to be more important than they really are. Old timers appropriately assessed the value of perceived importance. "I would like to buy him for what he's worth, and sell him for what he thinks he's worth." The image you project will either "endear" you to others or make you "an endurance" for others. The leader that communicates, "There are no 'big shots,' we're just all shot together" will hit his or her target, and will create a mutual admiration society in the process.

Self-Centered Deception

Self-importance minimizes the worth of others. It is an obsession that causes one to lose sight of the feelings and accomplishments of others. Self-centeredness devalues both subordinates and peers. Frequently, it is cloaked in verbiage that attests to the achievements of others, but focuses the attention on the arrogant leader's perceived successes. Competent subordinates will not be deceived; they will be insulted by the hypocrisy of the recognition. Arrogance that finds expression in self-adulation through the achievements of others solicits disdain and loss of respect.

Don't overlook the fact that you may need, at a later time, assistance from the very people you used as stepping-stones on your way up. If you ever have to descend, those same steps will be precarious. "What goes up must come down." The irony of fate, sometimes, seems to dictate that the paths you cross on the way down will be with those you were condescending to on your way up.

Leadership requires emotional stability. The danger of placing ill-prepared people in leadership roles is constant. You can ruin good people with a position. The first evidence that someone has been improperly placed is obsessive arrogance. Some people cannot handle leadership. More will be said later as we examine the curse of titles.

Assertiveness

Ability to Recognize

Assertiveness, effectively used, enhances "can do" leadership skills. Patricia Haddock, in *Leadership Skills for Women*, defined assertive behavior as active, direct, and honest, communicating an impression of self-respect and respect for others. It exemplifies direction. It says, "I can and will do it." In hiring, it is important to be able to identify unencumbered assertiveness which is simply the capability to act with boldness, self-confidence, and respect. It is not an obnoxious, overbearing, domineering, know-it-all, egotistical, rude behavior. It is not a verbose proclamation of self-worth or overstatement of one's ability. It takes an astute leader to discern the difference. You must be able to make a distinction between the individual that is assertive and the "smart aleck." The inability to do so will be costly because it will impact others.

A Personal Warning

If you are personally susceptible and easily impressed by egotistical rhetoric, you will be blinded to the shortfalls of those by whom you are deceived. Assertiveness, free of a self-serving agenda, is an invaluable leadership asset. Be alert to the fact that assertiveness and arrogance are a combustible mixture.

Intuition

Intuition is identified as the power or faculty of attaining direct knowledge or cognition, without evident rational thought and inference. It is invaluable, but it is not infallible. It has been identified as a two-edged sword. Just like first impressions, it is important, but may not be correct. As impressions are influenced by multiple factors including circumstances, personalities, and personal baggage, the intuition may also be influenced by subconscious factors. Your intuition will serve you well, but one miscalculation could drastically make a difference in your effectiveness as a leader.

Intuition is but one of many important tools in your toolbox. Let it serve you, but never let it control you. In your search for truth, subject your intuitive moments to close scrutiny. The following quote from an unknown source captures the peril of its misuse.

"The discoveries of intuition must always be supported by logic. In everyday life, as in science, intuition is a powerful but dangerous means of knowledge. It is sometimes difficult to distinguish it from illusion."

—Unknown

Titles

The impact a title will have on an individual can be unexpected and, at times, unpleasant. Titles, to some, are more important than financial rewards. They represent power, prestige, fame, and authority. All tenured leaders can report dismay over giving titles to individuals that simply could not handle them. "The position went to their head," and their personalities were drastically altered. The evidence glaringly reveals that the position appointment was inappropriate. Even though their work performance and expertise appeared to entitle them to assume a more prominent position, the maturity to assume the role never materialized. Contrarily, the position negatively impacted their work performance and peer relationships in the work place. A persistent preoccupation with a new title, position, or authoritative role will usually make the individual a casualty. The casualty is compounded by the fact that they most likely will be unable to return to their prior performance level in either their prior or reassigned role.

Some personalities become "control freaks" when given a title. Control freaks should be carefully monitored and their authority clearly defined. A person's aptitude to perform may not be compatible with their potential. If you value potential more than liability, you should expect the latter. Control freaks are obsessed with power and authority. Usually they demonstrate an ability to "know just enough to make them dangerous." They may practice intimidation, refuse to admit error, and be autocratic. Control freaks have a history of unscrupulous, deceptive, and disloyal behavioral patterns. Control freaks often create crises that require control.

> "Titles distinguish the mediocre, embarrass the superior, and are disgraced by the inferior."
>
> —George Bernard Shaw

Personal Hygiene

"Cleanliness is next to Godliness." I am not sure I ever fully understood the full intent of the message, but it seems to suggest good hygiene is a character issue. Poor grooming, bad breath, and body odor are worse than the "drips" of life. Fuzzy noses and ears with age will be a distraction to others. Balding and graying changes our grooming priorities. They reflect our values and self-worth. Personal grooming habits should be as normal as breathing for the professional leader.

Grooming either enhances or impedes our interactions with others. Our ability to communicate and interact with others is crucial to the leader's role, but communication can be impeded by negative impressions. Inattentiveness to grooming details can be extremely costly; especially when you consider that preventive measures are so inexpensive. *Dress for Success*, a few years ago, captured the imagination of the corporate world, and adherence to the guidelines, power ties and all, resembled religious fanaticism. Dress is now assessed based on what is appropriate and acceptable for your place of employment. Casual wear has made the work experience more relaxed, but there is a fine line between casual dress and inappropriate dress.

Profanity

Implications

Profanity has no leadership role. If vulgarity is your forte', or frequent expletives your choice for expression, expect others to experience communicative inhibitions. Offensive language is a violation of the rights of others. Respect and profanity are like oil and water. They are not compatible. Profanity never impressed anyone worth being impressed. It is a testimonial of a limited vocabulary and a verbalization of unresolved conflict.

Profuse profanity screams, "I'm in charge!" The language used is a contradiction of that message. The language expresses a personal struggle with life's frustrations, a temper out of control, or a learned habit that has become a psychological crutch. The issue is control. It is an oxymoron. The fear of a loss of control drives the behavior, but the behavior is a loss of control. A leader without self-control is ill-equipped to control the lives of others. Profanity is distasteful, offensive, unnecessary, and unprofessional. "Language is a window to the soul." It reveals who and what we are.

The following article was circulated years ago before profanity became an accepted motif for aspiring leaders. It may be a dated relic, but the relevance of truth persists.

Ten Reasons Why I Swear

1. It pleases mother so much.
2. It is a fine mark of manliness.
3. It proves I have self-control.

4. It indicates how clearly my mind thinks.
5. It makes my conversation pleasing to everyone.
6. It leaves no doubt in anyone's mind as to my good breeding.
7. It impresses people that I have more than an ordinary education.
8. It is an unmistakable sign of culture and refinement.
9. It makes me a very desirable personality among women and children in respectable society.
10. It is my way of honoring God who said,

"Thou shalt not take the name of the Lord your God in vain."

Outcome

Profanity as a leadership ploy hurts and victimizes people. "Sticks and stones may break my bones, but words will never hurt me." Physically this may be true, but emotionally words can, and do hurt. Words, once spoken, cannot be retrieved. Forgiveness may be begged and pardon pleaded, but memory lingers. Professional etiquette may even solicit a verbalized acceptance of an apology, but emotional hurt, still causes pain. Poor memory is the exception and not the rule with emotional hurt.

Simplicity

An Exquisite Virtue

There is virtue in simplicity. This work is written on the premise that this exquisite virtue cannot be ignored. Intrigue with academia and the use of academic expressions should be confined to the academic community. One of the definitions of academia is: "Very learned, but inexperienced in practical matters." Each professional field seems to zealously develop its own professional jargon to distinguish its exclusivity. I recall one disheartened congregant's assessment of the minister's demeanor and sermon delivery. "He is so heavenly minded, he is of no earthly good." Old timers used to speak of individuals who, "spoke above their heads" or "were not down to earth." Again, I remind you of the "KISS" rule. "Keep it simple stupid!"

Scholarly research and related dissertations are crucial to technological advancement and scientific research, but have limited relevance to life "where the rubber meets the road." An attempt to embellish practicality with academic trappings may impress a few, but will negatively impact effective communication. Remember, you are the leader of all, regardless of their academic level. Even his staunchest enemies recognized Jesus Christ as a master teacher, yet He spoke the language of a commoner. The simplicity of his message is profound. He spoke of nature and used practical illustrations from everyday life. This was the message His followers understood.

His message was delivered within, most likely, a radius of a hundred miles. Over two thousand years have passed since these simple lessons were delivered in a remote corner of the world, yet they continue to be discussed and debated on an international scale, as fervently as if the events occurred in our own lifetime.

Trust

The Con Artist!

The media frequently focuses on public trust issues and unscrupulous politicians, and corporate or public officials. The attention is justified and the scrutiny invaluable. History suggests people are gullible. The masses, learned and unlearned, are prey for the charismatic leader. All demonstrate a degree of receptiveness, but some are more naïve than others. Deception has no boundaries. Its tentacles are evident in every facet of society, from business to the political rostrum, to the pulpit. Deception becomes a way of life for many, and a professional trade for the con artist. Infatuation, even adoration, can easily be solicited by cunning charisma.

Most people want to believe the best of individuals. Cynics fear the worst from all. The tendency to believe the best of everyone is the better of these two possibilities. It is healthier to believe the best, while preparing for the worst. Naïve individuals hurt more deeply when disappointed by others. They perceive it to be a betrayal of trust. This level of trust is the power of the con artist. Error will always say, "Trust me."

Treasure Trust

The leadership role positions a person in a trust relationship. Treasure that trust. Trust is an awesome responsibility. It carries with it respect, admiration, reliance, and confidential disclosures. Don't be guilty of exploitation. Opportunistic practices that capitalize on the credulity of another's trust, or one's own contrived charm, will ultimately be exposed. Deceptive behavior, as a leader, can establish detrimental life-long patterns of mistrust, skepticism, and cynicism in the lives of those that are deceived.

Tough Times

When the going gets tough, and it will, the trust your subordinates have in you may be your only resource. Corporate downsizing, economic reversals, and cataclysmic events do occur. There are two valley episodes for every mountain top experience. Perhaps we should prepare accordingly. Regardless of their frequency, the loneliness of these events will require the leader to draw on the trust he or she has deposited in the minds and hearts of subordinates. The leader who chronically misrepresents the truth, is deceitful, or fails to make good on commitments is bankrupt. If the leader is neither trusted nor respected, their word is worthless. Past successes will be of no value and attempts at reconciliation will be suspect and overshadowed by distrust.

Trust and faith are two words that are used interchangeably. Both imply confidence in the credence of a story, person, or thing. The Biblical definition of faith is, "It is the substance of things hoped for and the evidence of things not seen." Please allow me to digress by proposing questions for thought. Is faith a prerequisite to trust, or is it a simultaneous experience? Does trust demonstrate a greater intensity of belief than faith? I recognize the questions proposed could all be contested and are subject to etymological scrutiny, but hopefully, they provoke thought to prepare us to consider the inspiration of faith, and the intensity of a persuasion that leads to trust.

You can by faith believe a chair will support your weight, but you do not act on that opinion until you place your weight in the chair. Faith does not understand; it leads to understanding. Is faith the inspiration that motivates action? This is awesome. Is trust then the conclusion that the chair will support your weight? Trust is placing your weight in the chair. Faith is the vehicle that leads to the culmination of a trust experience. As a leader, be sure the chair you offer is substantial to support your claims and the faith of those you lead.

Space

"Don't fence me in!" Step on an elevator and observe firsthand the dynamics of space. Individuals, non-verbally, communicate a claim to their space. The reluctance to make eye contact, the inhibition regarding casual conversation, body language, and the solitude of the person's demeanor says it all. It is imperative that personal space be respected and protected. Intrusion into another's space can be perceived at worst as threatening, and at best a violation of one's privacy. This natural reaction to close quarters provides invaluable insight. Individuals are emotionally divested of their personal dignity when forbidden adequate space. Their proximity to others can impede potential. Limited space suggests incarceration, and the implication of incarceration is restraint. Restraints limit potential.

The value you place on physical space for your subordinates is indicative of the value you place on the individual. Space is a priceless commodity. It is a personal issue that impacts performance and productivity. The importance of space and how individuals are allowed to stake their claim on their space is a costly oversight in the workplace. It will either enrich or deter working relationships. Work place planning must give preferential consideration to the creation of user friendly space. The pride one takes in their environment can energize their work. Individuals crammed into cramped quarters will ultimately give their emotions expression. It may be verbal or nonverbal, overt or covert, but it will happen. Leaders that are sensitive to a person's space criteria will enjoy the reciprocal rewards of that kindness.

Mentoring Maladies

Mentoring requires two participants. It requires a willing mentee and a qualified mentor. Individuals that have no desire to be mentored are not mentees. They are subjects of the system. Mentees must demonstrate pliancy. A mentor is defined as a wise and trusted counselor or teacher. The definition implies perimeters. The mentee's trust in the mentor, a desire to learn, and compliance with instruction is as important as knowledge and right motive is to the mentor. The labeling on the package may or may not reflect contents. Simply placing two people in static roles does not create a mentoring experience. Discernment of the capacity of an individual to be mentored reverts to the hiring process

The motive of the leader choosing to subscribe to a mentoring program must be right. The exclusivity of focus is crucial. Mentoring is an exercise to nurture people, not the leader's personal image. It is not a perfunctory exercise for either political correctness or image enhancement. Never use mentoring as a platform for self-exultation, personal grievances, or other agendas. The process does not lend itself to either egotism or autocratic practices.

Mentoring for the participant can be an invaluable experience that demonstrates the value of a nurturing relationship. Some individuals value mentoring more than others. Effective mentoring programs ingratiate reluctant participants. A mentoring process requires time, money, and patience. Presumptuous liberties that infringe on the mentee's comfort level will seriously flaw the process. Give individuals space, time, and a nurturing interest as they are introduced to growth opportunities through mentoring.

Mentoring euphoria must include a process to, for want of a better word, "credential" anyone assuming the role of a mentor. A mentor's skills must first be assessed. Character driven wisdom should demonstrate the skill to empathize and energize, while visualizing both needs and potential. Mentors should not be selected as public relations officers or promotional people for the executive in charge. The merits of the executive officer and the organization are best served when based upon substance, not hype. "Brown nosers" short circuit the mentoring process.

Mentoring can intrude into fragile areas of an individual's life. The trust required of the mentee mandates that unprincipled people be eliminated from the mentoring process. Integrity demands that the emotions and personal goals of an individual be respected at all costs. Individuals should never be exploited, manipulated, or subjected to mind games for personal gratification. There is no place for misguided egotism and the interjection of disconcerting baggage into the mentoring process.

Mission

"Window Dressing"

Mission statements give direction and capture imagination. Too often these statements are only cleverly designed clichés to make everyone feel good. Only people can breathe life into mission statements.

Mission statements without vision are little more than a figment of the imagination. The distinction between a mission statement and a vision is important. It has been said that a mission statement comes from the head; a vision comes from the heart.

The Best Example!

We number our days based on a calendar that reminds us of Christ's earthly existence. The mention of Christ's name brings immediate recognition, and the lessons He taught are still fervently followed. He assembled a small group of twelve and gave them his undivided attention. He personally trained them for three years. Some were learned, some unlearned, some were meek, some were quiet, and others were rambunctious or loud. The training they received focused exclusively on their personal growth.

He gave them a challenge when he selected them. He gave them their mission after he captured their hearts. The intensity of their training program made their mission statement a living force. Their commitment and vision was so intense, they did not flinch when given their awesome mission. This handful of followers had traveled with Him within no more than a hundred mile radius, yet His mission was mind boggling in scope. It was global! His mission was clear. Today, He receives international acclaim, recognition, and worship. Statements never performed a mission. Prepared people perform missions.

Stability

"A rolling stone gathers no moss." Stability by previous generations equated to the accumulation of tangible assets. Frequent moves were not in the equation. Old timers calculated three residential moves to be as costly as a fire. A series of events catapulted change in America. Permanent agricultural societies were prominent and mobility was limited. The nation quickly emerged and evolved from an industrial to a technological society. Rapid urbanization set this evolutionary process in motion. The speed of the transition left to the rusting remnants of industrialization the challenge of retooling for the inevitabilities of movement and change. Major corporations deemed the frequent movement of key employees a required stimulant. The general mobilization of society necessitated movement.

Stagnation can and does occur without stimulating movement, but movement without purpose is crippling to a stabilized work environment. An unstable environment will have a negative impact on productivity and assets. The propensity for change can override prudence. The burning embers of common sense truth will hopefully inspire calculated moves.

Flattery

I have chosen to treat flattery as a separate section, totally detached from discussions on truthfulness and lies. Flattery is defined as insincere or excessive praise. As individuals, we all positively respond to it and have been duped by those who practice it. It feeds the ego. Some individuals build a career based on their ability to flatter the right people. The common sense definition of flattery is "brown nosing." Flattery is a form of lying. Its intent is to deceitfully lead and mislead.

Two cautious considerations are worthy. First is the leader who chooses to flatter his followers to gain their allegiance. The second is the leader who easily succumbs to the flattery of those who prostitute themselves for payoff favors. Both are treacherous. Flattery has been described as a beautiful lie, but it will have ugly consequences. The leader who leads with flattery will discover the well will run dry. The question is, what to do for an encore? When flattery becomes the sole source of inspiration and motivation, the leader should expect fickle followers. Flattery used by followers for favors is more dangerous. The temptation of a leader to revel in personalized greatness is a welcomed target for deceitful followers. Some argue that flattery will get you anywhere. I argue flattery will take you nowhere.

Culture

Definition of culture: The behaviors and beliefs characteristic of a particular social, ethnic, or age group. The culture of an organization can be productive, unproductive, friendly, unfriendly, combative, forgiving, deceitful, suspicious, generous, stingy, prejudiced, industrious, lackadaisical, judgmental, oppressive, secretive, closed, or open. It depends on the leader. The culture is a reflection of the leader. The leader creates the environment. Nowhere is this more evident than in congregational gatherings. If the minister is outgoing, friendly, and caring, the congregation will replicate the behavior. Culture determines quality not quantity. It impacts every aspect of an organization's operation. Productivity, the attitude of staff, the spirit of cooperation, job satisfaction, and even physical safety are only a few of many possibilities. Cultural practices, if unhealthy, will jeopardize the organization and negatively impact every individual associated with it.

First impressions can be misleading. The true culture of an organization may be shrouded by superficial fluff. Individuals may project the image they perceive to be appropriate and necessary for job preservation, while in the presence of dysfunctional leadership. This façade internalizes frustration that cries for expression. Image building rhetoric, and the energy of the march to conformity's tune may muffle the sour notes that sound discord in the organization.

Culture is best discerned when leadership is not present. The absence of the leader acts as a disclosure statement revealing the fine print of covert unrest. Maladjusted behaviors thrive in the vacuum created by a leader's absence. The perimeters for acceptable behaviors are defined by the culture of the organization. Positive culture traits effectively contribute to an infrastructure that sustains organizational operations during times of leadership vacancies and change. Organizations that struggle, or have chronic negative behaviors in the absence of leadership have a culture problem.

The leader must assume full responsibility since the "buck stops with leadership." Leaders who develop a culture that stimulates misunderstandings, co-dependency, distrust, quarrels, and confusion, are responsible for the adversative outcomes that occur when they are absent from their leadership role. Micro-management by the leader will create a culture of co-dependency. Co-dependency generates insecurities that rely on an authority figure to provide solutions and direction for any and all difficulties that arise. When the authority figure is absent, individuals cannot function, and experience confusion and frustration. Micro-managers get their egos stroked by the dynamics of the co-dependent relationship.

The cop-out and rationalization for their failure is always, "When the cat's away, the mice will play." Some leaders even narcissistically convince themselves such disarray is proof positive that they are indispensable. The real dynamic at play is emotional release by employees who have pent up hostilities toward a system that stifles professional growth and job satisfaction. The opportunistic convenience of the leader's absence as a platform for destructive or lackadaisical behavior provides testimony of the leader's inability to stimulate a constructive culture. The issue is culture! The flaw is leadership!

Boards

The position of leadership will inevitably lead to an unpleasant encounter, at some level, with a governing board. Governing boards are comprised of diverse personalities and agendas that are often in conflict with the mission and success of the organization served. The composition of the mix can result in dynamic results, or it can create a counter productive dynamic. Individuals serve on boards for a variety of reasons. Commitment to a cause, recognition, prestige, perks, and power pursuits are common motivations. I suspect it is alarming how few board members serve on boards for altruistic reasons.

A functional board provides futuristic leadership, prevents administrative maladies, and sustains financial integrity to ensure the success of the organization they serve. Few board members fully comprehend their fiduciary role, or the legal implications of such a role. The board member who embraces these integral responsibilities will ensure the proliferation of the organization's mission.

The effectiveness or ineffectiveness of an individual member can impact the success or failure of the board. The success or failure of the organization is ultimately a reflection of the success or failure of the board. The power of one individual board member cannot be ignored. One verbose, self-serving board member can reek havoc, deter progress, and ultimately ensure failure if permitted the luxury of self-indulgence. Selfish purposes demonstrate the power of a single person. It is also true that one dynamic visionary can energize success. The effective leader will never underestimate the power of vocalized discord. Likewise, the successful leader will always respect the diversity of opinions regardless of the presentation style.

The leadership position that requires a board relationship presents unique challenges and a need for special insight. This role has a "Big Brother." Based on an organization's by-laws, the board may have the authority to critique, endorse, overrule, or negate planning objectives or administrative decisions. Malfunctioning boards run the full gamut. Some could care less about the organization; some focus on control, and others the "bottom line." Functional boards have a healthy involvement with the organization and are driven by what is best for the organization.

The successful leader will not only learn from board members, but will also learn about them. Their motivations, interests, life circumstances, failures, and successes are all influences that can and will impact their decision-making processes. Individual board members that have been highly successful in life have experienced the need to exercise liberty. They appreciate and respect autonomy. Generally, they have a propensity to be more generous with leadership liberty. They understand the need for it and the responsibilities attached to it.

Individual board members who have struggled with personal success in life may superimpose pent up hostility, consciously or subconsciously, on board decisions and their expectations for both the organization and the responsible leader. Disenchantment, the baggage of personal failure or an obsession for surrogate success, can be a measurable reflection of the intensity of their negative life experience. This insight can be invaluable to the astute leader.

Downsizing

The fluctuating fortunes of the market place, legislation, local economies, and internal deficiencies are only a few of a limitless number of adverse situations that demand reorganization and staff reductions. These inevitabilities require forethought. This may very well be the ultimate test for a leader. How it is conducted, the ability to empathize, and the support that is provided will be determining factors. Brevity is unwise for such a delicate subject, but space or time cannot do the subject justice in this publication. I submit a simplistic pattern for a complex issue. The plan should include:

1. Upon discovery, or even the suspicion of the possibility, initiate planning.

2. Never give staff "false hopes."
3. Prepare staff without creating unnecessary fear.
4. Provide full and public disclosure of cause.
5. Treasure the trust of affected staff in the process.
   a. Inform early and thoroughly.
   b. Preserve their dignity (confidentiality).
   c. Properly compensate them.
   d. Provide counseling and assistance.

Note: Downsizing should never be used to rid an organization of problematic employees. Employee problems should be resolved as a management issue.

The conclusion of the event is as crucial, if not more crucial than the event itself. Preliminary planning for this time frame must be twofold. It must address your personal needs as a leader and the needs of those impacted by the reduction. Planning should include the opportunity for peers in the workplace to process the event, but the procedure must be constructive and not a platform for disgruntled individuals to verbalize complaints under the guise of hurt.

The focus for the moment is resiliency and the ability to adapt to change, neither of which is possible if negative connotations are belabored. Prolonged attention and extended discussions will energize disruptive reactions that result in speculations and gossip. Initial anxieties and fears will be rekindled, giving new life to old embers that should have long been extinguished. It is best to "let sleeping dogs lie." Inspiration that provides direction is the shortest route to acceptance and recovery.

The leader's credibility, leadership style, trustworthiness, and competencies will surface in the experience. If the leader has neither, there will be a devastating "trickle down" effect.

Community

Community is the fulfillment of a conceptualized truth. It provides a support system for personal enrichment. It is a natural process that emanates from a principle that values people and enjoys relationships. The premise that truth originates from God gives community a divine birthright. It is important to observe the principle at work in the early followers of Christ. It was perfected during his life and energized by the mission he gave them. A succession of followers perpetuated this spirit of community. The dynamic of the building of religious community is so powerful, it enjoys a covenant warranty.

The concept was introduced to the secular world when leaders began to recognize its potential. The spirit of community came into vogue as a workplace phenomenon. Community is realized when individuals embrace principles that build interpersonal and cooperative assemblages of common persuasions.

Proponents of its potential for secular entities will be well served to solidify personal philosophies that can embrace the truth principles that sustain the philosophy of true community. Acknowledgement of its origin energizes the principle from which the philosophy emerges. The principle was pursued and zealously taught by Christ during his earthly ministry. His goal for His followers, as well as His prayer, was that they might experience oneness. It has been suggested that the only unanswered prayer of Christ during his earthly ministry was his prayer that true community (oneness) would be experienced by all of his followers. A sense of community did exist in the small quarrelsome extended family of followers that zealously embraced his teachings. The spirit of community, born through adversity, constructive confrontation, and commitment reached full fruition immediately after Christ's departure from earth. This handful of followers grew rapidly from one hundred twenty, to three thousand, to five thousand, because they had all things in common. They generated a movement that spanned the globe, and all of Christendom embraced, theoretically, his teaching on the importance of "community."

Lip service only manifests the fallacy of practice without persuasion. Hypocrisy disables the potential for true community. Community is not taught, imposed, or legislated; it is experienced. True community has focus, is not intrusive, can be led, and is void of ego-centric motives. The ultimate focus, from a scriptural standpoint, was to establish an intimate community for created mortals in their pursuit of restored access to the Creator. The intensity of the Creator's desire for a restoration of paradise lost (communion with God in Eden's Garden) can only be assessed by the sacrificial offering he made.

John 3:16
> "For God so loved the world, that He gave His only begotten Son, that whosoever believeth in Him should not perish, but have everlasting life."
>
> —King James Version

Divine principles work! Truth is immutable, even though those that are less than honorable may misuse the principles. The seed of truth that espouses the principle can be compromised, improvised, embellished, and deceitfully implemented. The truth contained in them can even inadvertently appear to validate error in a questionable practice. The principles of true community, because they are truth, can support any cause, be they noble or self-serving. Misuse of the principle is another intrusion into the divine.

The perpetrator who uses divine principles to either promote their personal philosophies, or selfishly benefit from their misuse, must recognize their accountability to those they lead. The implementation of the concept of community, when void of its divine intention, should have qualifiers and clearly defined perimeters. Community, in itself, is not a substitute for spiritual meaning in life. It is not group therapy. It is not a support group. It is not a surrogate family, nor should it ever have personalized motives. Integrity demands that we identify our motives. Deceptive motives are easily identified.

> "If it walks like a duck, quacks like a duck, flies like a duck, and swims like a duck, it is a duck."

Respect

Community is fragmented when self-love prohibits caring concern for others. The distance between selfishness and selflessness is a chasm and will require patience and self-discipline. Selflessness is only possible when an individual is capable of exercising self-love (self-respect). It is used as the standard by which we should measure our respect for others. Self-respect creates a healthy self-esteem. It internalizes a value system that qualifies one to respect others. The germination of this truth can be evidenced through obedience to two basic commands that summarize all the teachings of the Bible. Love God, and love your neighbor as yourself.

Matthew 22:37-40

> "Jesus said unto him, Thou shalt love the Lord thy God with all thy heart, and with all thy soul, and with all thy mind. This is the first and great commandment. And the second is like unto it. Thou shalt love thy neighbor as thyself. On these two hang all the law and the prophets."
>
> —King James Version

Community is interdependency at work. Interdependency cannot exist without respect.

Caution!

The principle of community building, when applied to any group or organization creates an enriching growth process. The pretense of community building as a subterfuge for group therapy, pop psychology, or psychoanalysis will negatively impact community, and subject some individuals to emotional stress. Any attempt to use a therapeutic approach to community building will be perceived by some as deceptive, and will undermine the integrity of the community building experience.

If the organization is not a faith tradition community, the leader must be cautious not to allow the process to evolve into a pseudo-religious experience, and it should never, under any circumstances, be considered a surrogate family relationship. Faith and family traditions are both sacred and personal, and should be respected. The integrity of the building of a spiritual community, with faith traditions and dogma, is reserved for churches, Christian movements, and religious organizations. Any perceived intrusion into the value-based systems of faith or family will create resistance.

The principles of community building are the foundational stones upon which Christian relationships are formed and sustained, but they are also applicable to any organization, including the workplace. Its origin does not suggest that the "spirit" of Christian community should create spiritual elitism or be confined to a religious organization. The "spirit" of one's faith tradition, if genuine, will have a positive influence on every relationship encounter.

Extreme Abuse

Misuse of community principles, when construed for the purpose of creating pseudo-religious communities or surrogate families, can create cultic relationships. The principles can be used opportunistically, or for self-serving purposes. Cultic practices isolate, indoctrinate, and dictate lifestyles. Community is not an exclusive relationship; it is an inclusive relationship that respects individuals and promotes a non-judgmental liberty that allows members the freedom, opportunity, and encouragement to expand their relationships within the framework of any group affiliation.

Exclusivity is fertile soil for cultic germination. Cults are born when individuals forming a community stop learning, stop growing, and are either overtly or covertly forced to internalize the spoon-fed, self-serving perceptions of unscrupulous leaders. Restraints that prohibit an individual from learning and exploring truth, or that legislate relationships, result in isolation. The ultimate offense of isolation is when information is neither questioned nor examined. Isolation and exclusivity fertilizes the inbreeding of contaminated truth.

Christ was severely criticized by the religious leaders of his day because he associated with "sinners." His followers envisioned a religious cloister, yet he practiced visionary outreach through community to help hurting people. The fact is, individuals that are conflicted or in crisis are most in need of emotional support and caring concern. Judgmental attitudes, preconceived conclusions, and exclusion based on personal agendas create co-dependency within a community.

An individual may experience the spirit of active community in multiple organizations and groups. These may involve the work place, community organizations, civic, or religious groups. No single affiliation should infringe upon the integrity of the other. On some occasions, when there is a consensus of purpose, one may often compliment another. Any community that prohibits multiple participation in one or more communities should be suspect and avoided. Any leader that dictates the scope of personal relationships is dubitable, and his or her motivations should be carefully examined.

"The meeting of two personalities is like the
contact of two chemical substances;
if there is any reaction,
both are transformed."

—Carl J. Jung

"Leadership,
like swimming,
cannot be learned
by reading
about it."

—Henry Mintzberg

SUMMARY

This book is an unfinished work; it is a work in progress. I invite you to research your own resources of "common sense" and apply truth principles to your leadership role. There is a pervasive presence of "unsophisticated wisdom" available to every reader, based on your specific geographic region or cultural heritage. The diverse cultures of differing ethnic groups have rich traditions of "unsophisticated wisdom." Comprehension of truth seems to be best communicated through simplistic expressions that depict truth in sound logic.

America is a nation of immigrants founded upon Judaeo-Christian values. The premise of these values is "truth." This does not suggest these values were judiciously embraced, or that they dominated the course of events in either faith traditions or American history. It is true that truth, in embryonic form, survives to find expression and understanding through prolific, simplistic "common sense" sayings. They provide direction, and are in many cases an invaluable source of strength to overcome the adversities of life.

Our legacies emerge from ignorance, learning, poverty, plenty, war, persecution, slavery, and prevailing prejudices. Regardless of heritage, life experiences dictate reality. Our diligence to comprehend truth determines life's choices. Those choices result in the quality of life we experience. We will never realize or fully appreciate the impact these homespun increments of truth have on our co-existence with one another.

Every leader is encouraged to academically research and develop credible leadership skills. But this pursuit must include an appreciation of "common sense," and commitment to it. I have, in this book, attempted to challenge the reader to access this overlooked resource. I challenge you to investigate "common sense" principles and identify the divine truth that energizes them. I encourage you to be bold enough to eliminate the secular and sacred "mind-sets" that prohibit divine influence in your interactions with life events.

Embrace Simplicity

"If it sounds too good to be true, it is." The simplicity of this example doesn't do justice to the profound truth contained in it. This is true with the sayings, lessons, and observations that subconsciously or consciously molded our lives. They, collectively, are a dynamic resource. The samplings of stories, sayings, and allegories quoted in this book capture the essence of truth. These common recitations illustrate unencumbered, "unsophisticated wisdom."

I have not scratched the surface, let alone exhausted the sayings, folk wisdom, allegories, or examples that allowed you to "pull yourself up by your own bootstraps." You alone control your resources. Only you, from your own experience and exposure, can apply your recollections of "unsophisticated wisdom" to your role as a leader. I can assure you, if the applicability of truth principles in common sense was a product, I could give a money back guarantee. Truth principles do work. The decision to act on these principles is personal, and it is your choice.

Assume Leadership

Take the Lead!

"It is lonely at the top," and the "buck does stop there." Decision-making is a lonely task, but as a leader, you must lead. I have read with interest much on the nomadic lifestyle of the shepherds, and have been intrigued by their commitment to care. They jeopardize their own safety in the care of the flock. They alone are responsible for the well being of the sheep. The health, safety, and welfare of the flock are contingent on their leadership skills. The shepherd's familiarity, care, association, and presence with his flock make him recognizable. The scriptures remind us of this phenomenon. The sheep hear the voice of the shepherd and follow. This relationship is more than a learned response through training, it is an association dynamic with the shepherd. The flock identifies with the shepherd and follows. Where the flock moves, how they are cared for, and what they are subjected to, is the responsibility of the shepherd. This requires the capability to make good decisions, and lead.

I have yet to read of a shepherd who gathered his flock and took a vote of the sheep to determine which pasture or what hillside they would select for grazing. Proactive leadership nurtures, provides direction, and protects the growth process. This leadership role is not dictated; it is earned in the long hours of care. It is important to remember, "the pasture is always greener on the other side," and the sheep that persists in choosing their own direction will always be problematic.

There are some choices that only the leader can make. The leader is solely responsible for leadership directives. In Chapter One, "getting the horse to drink" was the desired outcome. Your outcome is contingent on your process. The process begins with the trip to the watering trough. If the process is flawed, the outcome will be flawed.

The distinctive work of the leader is evidenced in the fact that leadership is always confronting problems. The ability to address difficulty is the mark of true leadership. This necessity of leadership is contingent on the inevitability of a role need to make difficult decisions.

Take the Bull by the Horns!

"When the going gets tough, the tough gets going." No one has ever suggested that leadership is an easy task. Leadership is an awesome, but rewarding experience. In difficult times of adversity you will discover that the greater the difficulty, the greater the reward. To use rodeo vernacular, "If the horse don't buck, the ride don't count." Regardless of the leadership role, when people don't understand you, purposely misrepresent you, or fail to trust you, your ability to lead will be the real test.

It can be overwhelming to realize you have a personal responsibility to lead those who do not want to be led, or lack confidence in your ability to lead. This irony emphasizes the importance of simplistic truth. You will find the accessibility of "unsophisticated wisdom" a welcomed resource. Resources that are untapped are meaningless. "Impression without expression leads to depression." Effective leadership requires commitment, dedication, and action. Proactive action is always more productive than reactive action.

Build People

Build On Strengths

Whether you supervise two, or two hundred people, whether your organization is non-profit or for profit, leadership principles are the same. "People building" is what leadership is all about. As a leader of people, you have multiple responsibilities and should have a singular commitment to every person you supervise. You must identify strengths, accept mistakes, create growth, and provide liberty for the growth experience. Individuals must be empowered to be powerful. They must be motivated to claim ownership.

Stimulate Learning

Successful organizations must be focused on continual improvement. It has been suggested that continuous improvement requires continuous learning. This is not an "organizational happening;" it is a consensus of individual need, and then a commitment to the learning process. Willing learners grow rapidly. Rapid personal growth spawns an exhilarating pattern of organizational growth. People growth empowers organizational growth. Dr. Peter Singe in his book entitled *The Fifth Discipline* coined the phrase, "The Learning Organization."

> "A learning organization is an organization skilled at creating, acquiring, and transferring knowledge, and at modifying its behavior to reflect new knowledge."
>
> —David A. Garvin

Build Unity

The "body concept" in the newly birthed Christian church characterized its organizational structure. This logic used the anatomy of the physical body. It stressed the importance of every body member and the relevance of each to the whole. Each member is important, each has a specific role to achieve, and the failure or deficiency of any will negatively impact all. The physical body is vibrant because it is a living organism. Organizations, if dynamic and energized, must function as living organisms. The independent strengths and the interdependent relationship of the members form a cohesive, energized unit. The human body, based on the function of each member, operates as a singular unit. Every member has a role to fill and each must depend on each other. Each has a role to fill, and each must depend on the other. Leadership requires "body building" if the organization is to be successful.

Teamwork

You build on consensus, even though there are decisions only the leader can make. Build on collective knowledge and strength. Synergy is dynamite! Creative, liberated managers and teams are imperative if organizations are healthy. Teamwork stimulates collective ownership, and ownership ensures accountability. "People power" makes things happen.

I do; you watch.
I do; you help.
You do; I help,
You do; I watch,
You know!
We do together as a team.

—Rusty Caldwell

Focus

Duplicity in leadership assignments confuses staff and dilutes directives. The leader's role and the role of subordinate managers or delegated work teams must be clearly defined. The scope of authority and mission must be clear. All must then be empowered to perform their identified roles. The leader must be willing to relinquish control to allow subordinates to effectively perform.

Micro-management is an insult to competent managers; it creates confusion, and blurs the lines of responsibility. Such a practice is reminiscent of the distasteful two-headed sideshows in carnivals of yesteryear. Undefined leadership is an unproductive oddity. People who understand the scope of their authority, and are permitted to exercise it, will be the foundational stones upon which any organization is built. Once they have been told what to do and why they are to do it, let them do it.

W. Edward Deming's challenge to management leadership consisted of:

1. An openness to trust employees
2. A willingness to delegate
3. A readiness to get out of the way instead of micromanaging
4. Assuming the role of leader instead of trying to direct behavior
5. Giving employees the tools to do the job

The failure to have a consistent criterion for managers and teams under your leadership will always be counterproductive.

Build On Inspiration

The Mission

Any organization must be inspired to act upon its mission. An army arrested by rest, an organization in limbo or disarray, an entity without vision for growth, or a church whose congregants or leader are not committed to ministry serve to illustrate this dilemma. All have the potential to create a feeding frenzy of self-destruction. An army must have a battle plan for conquest, and act upon it. An organization must have a defined objective for productivity, and produce. A church must have a mission of ministry, and minister.

Uninspired individuals are inactive individuals. Inactive individuals are bored individuals, and bored individuals create their own excitement. If not focused on a challenging mission, or if not provided appropriate direction, boredom's mischief will negatively critique individuals, programs, and initiatives. Boredom is no respecter of persons or institutions. The end result is that the critique becomes a self-generated, fulfilled prophecy. Even casual critiques have the potential to spawn malicious conclusions. The ability to criticize is the only credentialing required for the futility of this destructive conduct. Someone has suggested that it doesn't take a college degree or even a high school diploma to complain. In fact, one can be just "plain dumb" and complain. Boredom breeds malcontents!

Mobilize Movement!

If the scope of one's personal challenge is so limited that it is organizationally internalized, it will feed on criticism, complaints, and invalid judgmental assessments. The very fact the prerogative to judge usurps divine authority intensifies the potential for harm. The absurdity of this presumptuous action, and its inevitable outcome, intensifies the degenerative process.

Such a miscarriage of justice is most vividly evidenced in the one movement thought to be immune. Using the analogy of a marching army, it has been said that Christian movements are the only armies that ever shoot their wounded.

Inspiration's outcome will always be, busy people. Busy people are focused, energized, and happy. The complacency of Biblical Israel to pursue its mission immobilized their divine, promised objective. Fear, presumptuous conclusions, and exaggerated fond memories of bondage benefits led to internal strife. Internal strife prohibited occupation of the promised land, and ultimate dispersion.

The peril of lethargic idleness is documented in secular and sacred history. Another classic Biblical account vividly illustrates this point. The nation of Israel was at war and, its king is on the rooftop of his palace, removed from the mission, and lustfully observing another's wife. His disengagement and inactivity created an environment that led to an adulterous affair with the wife of a choice soldier, and then murder to conceal his dastardly act. King David's momentary encounter with idleness resulted in a lifetime of misery. "An idle mind is the devil's workshop."

"Most people stare up the steps rather than step up the stairs."
—Unknown

Value Humility

Humility is the quality or state of being humble. A person that is humble is not proud, haughty, arrogant, or pretentious. The reiterations in this book regarding self-centered egotism are purposeful reinforcements to prepare the successful leader for his or her greatest struggle. The likelihood they will be victimized by their own success, or perceived success, is their greatest challenge.

The press and the general public want, and seem to need, heroic leaders. The press habitually creates infallible heroes that are fuel for sensational, marketable newsprint for future editions. The thirst for scandal and the scrutiny of a gullible, unforgiving, hypocritical general public energizes this dynamism. The superficiality of an adoring public that initially accepted foolish hype, fabrications, and misinformation is evidenced when the same public seems to find gratification in scandalizing the hypothetical hero. The press is motivated by profit margins. The general public is intrigued and motivated by the displayed weaknesses of the rich and famous. Could it be that the vulnerability of the successful provides solace to the personally perceived inadequacies or failures of those less recognized or accomplished? Just remember, your moment of fame resides in a "glass house," and one well-aimed stone at a character flaw can shatter a lifetime of dreams.

The failures or misfortunes of leaders are often the result of over-confidence and a perception of infallibility. A leader's downfall commences when the leader begins to believe his or her own press releases. Adulation, power, fame, and the fringe benefits of success can readily change an individual's value system. Success can cause one to assume he or she is exempt from the rules of the general public or subordinates. It can formulate a false sense of immunity. It affirms the leader's personal misconceptions of perceived wisdom, skill, and accomplishments.

Success, as a general rule, is predicated on a person's ability. Often success is also the result of an individual being at the right place at the right time, and doing the right thing to accomplish the desired outcome. Circumstances and the subsequent dynamics of a natural chain of events may have contributed more to the successful outcome than the skill of the leader.

The susceptibility and likelihood of a leader being victimized by self-held perceptions of greatness is the leader's supreme challenge. The leader must be able to "keep both feet on the ground" while reaching for the stars. The graveyard of potential superstars is filled with those who could not handle success. Any position of leadership, regardless of the career field, is at risk. The carcasses of the shattered lives and dreams of leaders who discovered fame to be a fleeting illusion litter history's path. Testimonials reveal they were betrayed by their own deceptions and misconceptions of success.

Again the spiritual dimension of our susceptibilities are repeatedly addressed with Biblical sternness and simplicity. The Bible is filled with admonitions, illustrations, biographies, stories, and lessons that portray the warnings and inevitabilities of delusions of grandeur.

Proverbs 8:13
    "The fear of the Lord is to hate evil: pride, and arrogancy,
    and the evil way, and the forward mouth, do I hate."
                                            —King James Version

Proverbs 16:18
> "Pride goeth before destruction. And an haughty spirit before a fall."
>
> —King James Version

Perhaps some concluding practical reiterations regarding personal compliments would be helpful for your consideration:

1. Don't accept all the compliments you receive to be factual.
2. Don't use compliments to get others to reciprocate.
3. Don't fail to acknowledge a compliment.
4. Don't underestimate the power of a compliment.
   a. When you receive a compliment – appreciate it; don't misuse it.
   b. When you give a compliment – mean it; don't use it.

It's Biblical

Wisdom is a Biblical theme; it is described and explored by successive writers of the sacred text. Wisdom is never synonymous with academic learning; it probes philosophic issues that determine the quality of one's life. It finds expression in simplistic practicalities. It is valued, admonished, and desirable; it is not imposed; it is proposed. The learned and the unlearned were astonished by Christ's lesson plan. His application of common sense logic to the profound issues of life energized wisdom in his followers.

When selecting his protégés, he did not pursue the gifted or the learned. He did not choose academic achievers from the rabbinical schools of his day. He looked for teachable subjects with integrity and courage. He selected twelve to be mentored. Of the twelve, He focused particular attention on three. He appears to have personally coached them, as successors, to provide mission leadership. John Maxwell in *Developing the Leaders Around You* said, "There is no success without a successor."

Christ's mission would have been thwarted on the threshold of its birth had he not mentored others. His premeditated course of action is clear:

1. He selected twelve individuals to mentor.
2. He gave them a challenge to partner with him.
3. He had a personal interest in their welfare.
4. He used their mistakes as learning opportunities.
5. He mentored them for three years.
6. He appeared to personally coach three of the twelve.
7. He assessed their role readiness.
8. He prepared them for success.
9. He informed them of inevitable hardships.
10. He defined their mission.
11. He left them to carry it out.
12. They succeeded!

"Good equippers do it like Jesus did it: recruit twelve, graduate eleven, and focus on three."

—Lynn Anderson

The chronology of the timing of the Mission Statement is worthy of note.

Leave a Legacy

Departures from positions of leadership for most leadership roles are routine events. The event and subsequent aftermath provides insight into the departing leader's competencies. Some organizations disintegrate, while others thrive with growth. Both are reflections of the level of leadership skill. The delicate balance required to seize the moment, in either scenario, is the greatest challenge of new leadership.

Caution is advised. Departing leaders assume differing mind-sets regarding their successors. Some leaders measure personal success by the speedy demise of their successor. If the successor fails, it seems to affirm their worth and abilities. Verbalized delight in the failure of others carries the connotation of an internalized sadistic spoof. Others may simply be jealous over the successes of successors. These successes could be deemed a threat to their own achievements. Such behaviors often disclose insecurities and apprehensions of perceived shortcomings, or fears that failures will be discovered.

Likewise, incoming leaders should exercise caution. Assess strengths and weaknesses before acting. Build on strengths, and be attentive to giving credit where credit is due. Address weaknesses, and avoid needless criticism of your predecessor. I remind you that criticism of a predecessor never fixed a problem or contributed to a successful resolution.

There is always room for improvement. The most proficient of organizations has room for growth and, in fact, will stagnate without it. Vacancies provide opportunities to build upon the successes of predecessors. The expertise to take success and make it more successful takes more creativity, but it will distinguish you as a leader.

Organizations are also fraught with unknown debilitating discoveries. Skeletons can come out of the closet. These, too, are opportunities for new leadership. The challenge may be greater, but the rewards can be sweeter. The shortest route to credibility is the demonstrated ability to enact immediate change. Positive change, due to corrective action, will strengthen your ability to lead in a new environment.

Departing leaders' abilities are best affirmed by the successes of their successors. The greatest testimonial to your success is the effectiveness and longevity of the positive outcomes that occur after your departure. The most enduring testimony to your success as a leader is the strength of the infrastructure you bequeath your successor. Every leader should aspire to leave a legacy of perpetual success. Longevity equates to strength and durability. Leaders should strive to leave a living legacy! The legacy you leave will determine two destinies; yours, and those you have led.

Redundancy

I have intentionally restated several themes in differing chapters of the book. The purpose is to demonstrate that truth permeates every aspect of the leader's role. The leader must be honest, have credibility, not be egotistical, and understand that some actions can cause self-destruction. The roadway to calamity begins with a single step. Most successful leaders who encountered an untimely demise, did so because they perceived their status to be privileged. Those chosen by Jesus Christ argued over position and status regarding who would sit where in His Kingdom. Christ took a basin of water and a towel and washed their feet to illustrate servant leadership. Stature in the people building business is predicated on one's ability to serve those that are led.

Every leader is only one precarious step from a career ending calamity. Those that have been casualties simply underestimated the impact of one insignificant infraction that opened a "Pandora's Box" of more flagrant unauthorized liberties. Successful leaders generate their own make-believe world that makes them immune to reality and subsequent consequences. The frequency of published reports in the local and national news media of scandals involving politicians, power brokers, clergymen, television evangelists, teachers, ranking military officials, and chief executives verify the need for redundancy. It appears someone isn't listening!

The repetition of references to egoism emphasizes its importance. Life, and our interactions with others, is all about egos. We travel through life staking out territory for ourselves. The ills of life, our frustrations, unacceptable deeds, greed, anger, and even crime are birthed in one's ego. What can I get for myself? How can I bring attention to myself? How can I make myself feel or look better? No one will go unpunished who offends me! The beat goes on. I will go so far as to suggest that all evil originates in the ego. The pursuit of Adam and Eve to gain knowledge was stimulated by the possibility of becoming gods. History, I believe, will prove me right.

Ego-driven motives evolve subtly. Chronic and frequent practices result in mental and/or physical implications. As infants in the cradle, we develop strategies to have others meet our every need. A leadership position can be the grand finale of this objective, due to the acclaim and recognition associated with the role. Some serve life sentences imprisoned by their own egos.

Without discipline, our egos will run amuck! Submission and discipline are the antidotes. The followers of Jesus forsook all to follow him. The greatest struggle in life is the forfeiture of things that embellish what we hope to be. We all have a daily encounter with our own egos. John the Baptizer, as saints who followed, recognized that things would distract him from his mission.

John 3:30
   "He must increase, but I must decrease."
                                    —King James Version

"Experts say the average person, in a lifetime, influences ten thousand other people. Those in leadership positions influence many, many more. Consequently, leadership carries an incredible responsibility. Leaders need to make certain they're headed in the right direction."

—Zig Ziglar

"There
are three classes
of men—
lovers of wisdom,
lovers of honor,
lovers of gain."
—Plato

"If plain sense makes sense,
we should seek no other sense,
lest we create nonsense."
—Unknown

EPILOGUE

In Chapter One, I identified the pursuit of "common sense" as a quest. The motive must be pure in the search for wisdom. King Solomon valued wisdom more than wealth. The pureness of his motive brought him wisdom, honor, wealth, and power. An ancient world beat a path to his doorstep to marvel at his wisdom and wealth.

I Kings 3:3-13
"And Solomon loved the Lord, walking in the statutes of David his father: only he sacrificed and burnt incense in high places. And the king went to Gibeon to sacrifice there: for that was the great high place: a thousand burnt offerings did Solomon offer upon the altar. In Gibeon the Lord appeared to Solomon in a dream by night: and God said, Ask what I shall give thee. And Solomon said, Thou hast shewed unto thy servant David my father great mercy, according as he walked before thee in truth, and in righteousness, and in uprightness of heart with thee; and thou hast kept for him this great kindness, that thou hast given him a son to sit on his throne, as it is this day. And now, O Lord my God, thou hast made thy servant king instead of David my father: and I am but a little child: I know not how to go out or come in. And thy servant is in the midst of thy people which thou hast chosen, a great people, that cannot be numbered nor counted for multitude. Give therefore thy servant an understanding heart to judge thy people, that I may discern between good and bad: for who is able to judge this thy so great a people? And the speech pleased the Lord, that Solomon had asked this thing. And God said unto him, Because thou hast asked this thing, and hast not asked for thyself long life; neither hast asked riches for thyself, nor hast asked the life of thine enemies;

but hast asked for thyself understanding to discern judgment; Behold, I have done according to thy words: lo, I have given thee a wise and an understanding heart; so that there was none like thee before thee, neither after thee shall any arise like unto thee. And I have also given thee that which thou hast not asked, both riches, and honor: so that there shall not be any among the kings like unto thee all thy days."

—King James Version

The purity of Solomon's motive is evident in his desire for leadership wisdom.

1. His humility – He knew he didn't have all the answers.
2. His truthfulness – He admitted his weakness – He was honest with himself and others.
3. His priorities – He was in the people business for the benefit of the people, not for self-serving reasons.

The wisdom of Solomon was sought by royalty, but could be understood by a commoner. I would be remiss not to include the one example that best portrays his mastery of common sense logic.

I Kings 3:16-28
"Then came there two women, that were harlots, unto the king, and stood before him. And the one woman said, O my lord, I and this woman dwell in one house; and I was delivered of a child with her in the house. And it came to pass the third day after that I was delivered, that this woman was delivered also: and we were together; there was no stranger with us in the house, save we two in the house. And this woman's child died in the night; because she overlaid it. And she arose at midnight, and took my son from beside me, while thine handmaid slept, and laid it in her bosom, and laid her dead child in my bosom. And when I rose in the morning to give my child suck, behold, it was dead: but when I had considered it in the morning, behold, it was not my son, which I did bear. And the other woman said, nay; but the living is my son, and the dead is thy son. And this said, No; but the dead is thy son, and the living

is my son. Thus they spake before the king. Then said the king, The one saith, This is my son that liveth, and the other saith, Nay; but thy son is the dead, and my son is the living. And the king said, Bring me a sword. And they brought a sword before the king. And the king said, Divide the living child in two, and give half to the one, and half to the other. Then spake the woman whose the living child was unto the king, for her bowels yearned upon her son, and she said, O my lord, give her the living child, and in no wise slay it. But the other said, Let it be neither mine nor thine, but divide it. Then the king answered and said, Give her the living child and in no wise slay it: she is the mother thereof. And all Israel heard of the judgment which the kind had judged; and they feared the king: for they saw that the wisdom of God was in him, to do judgment."

—King James Version

Jeremiah 9:23-24
"Thus saith the Lord, Let not the wise man glory in his wisdom, neither let the mighty man glory in his might, let not the rich man glory in his riches: But let him that glorieth glory in this, that he understandeth and knoweth me, that I am the Lord which exercise lovingkindness, judgment, and righteousness, in the earth: for in these things I delight, saith the Lord."

—King James Version

The scope of America's role in the international community could not have been visualized by our founding fathers. The exclusivity of America's Judeo-Christian heritage is now negated by an influx of multicultural faith traditions. The challenge of a democratic society with subsequent rights and religious diversity has introduced new debates on religious pluralism. We are a nation of diverse immigrants.

This fact should not inhibit or diminish the practice of Biblio-centric principles. It establishes the need for a common denominator. In recent years, there has been a tendency for corporations to introduce, and sometimes mandate eastern euphoric spiritual exercises into the work place to enhance productivity, stimulate work place morale, and make individuals feel better about themselves. Feelings and truth may or may not be compatible.

"I never give them hell;
I just tell the truth,
And they think it's hell."
—Harry Truman

Philosophically, the nirvanas of religious practices may or may not embrace Biblical truth. In some cases, they are imitations of truth. Experiential adherence to divine principles will prevent the need for supplemental sources of inspiration. Any and all faith traditions must be respected, but none should be imposed on subordinates.

"True leadership
must be for the benefit
of the followers,
not the
enrichment
of the leaders."
—Robert Townsend

"Some people
live their
whole lives
just around the
corner
from the world of
truth."
—Carl F.H. Henry

ACKNOWLEDGEMENTS

BOOKS RELATED TO LEADERSHIP

Ambrose, Delorese, Ed.D. *Healing the Downsized Organization*. New York: Harmony Books, 1996

Anderson, Lynn. *They Smell Like Sheep*. West Monroe, Louisiana: Howard Publishing Company. 1997

Boone, Louis E. *Quotable Business*. New York: Random House, 1992 Champy, James. Reengineering Management. New York: Harper Business, 1996

Covey, Stephen R. *Principle-Centered Leadership*. New York: Simon & Schuster, 1992

Dobyns, Loyd, and Clare Crawford-Mason. *Thinking About Quality*. New York: Times Books, 1994

Fishkin, Gerald Loren, Ph. D. *American Dream, American Burnout How to Cope When It all Gets to Be Too Much*. United States of America: Loren Publications, 1994

Gordon, Dr. Thomas. *Leader Effectiveness Training*, L.E.T. United States of America: Wyden Books, 1977

Guiness, Os. *Time for Truth*, Grand Rapids, Michigan: Baker Books, 2000 Hammer, Michael, and Steven A. Stanton. The Reengineering Revolution. New York: Harper Business, 1995

Hind, James F. *The Heart & Soul of Effective Management*. Wheaton, Illinois: Victor Books, 1989

Holton, Bil, Ph.D. *Leadership Lessons of Robert E. Lee*. New York: Gramercy Books, 1995

Jones, Laurie Beth. *Jesus CEO*. New York: Hyperion, 1995

Kotter, John P. *The Leadership Factor*. New York: The Free Press, 1988

Maxwell, John C. *Developing the Leader Within You*. Nashville, Tennessee: Thomas Nelson Publishers, 1193

Rush, Myron. *Management: A Biblical Approach*. Wheaton, Illinois. Victor Books: 1988

Schlessinger, Dr. Laura and Rabbi Stewart Vogel. *The Ten Commandments*. New York: Cliff Street Books, 1998

Sheehy, Gail. Character, *America's Search for Leadership*. New York: William Morrow & Company Inc., 1988

Solomon, Muriel. *Working With Difficult People.* Paramus, New Jersey: Prentice Hall, 1990

Sveiby, Karl Erik. *The New Organizational Wealth.* San Francisco, CA: Berett-Kohler Publishers, Inc., 1997

Vaughn, David J. *Give Me Liberty.* General Editor George Grant. Nashville, TN: Cumberland House Publishing, Inc., 1997

Wilkes, C. Gene. *Jesus on Leadership.* Wheaton, Illinois: Tyndale House Publishers, Inc., 1998

COMMENTS

"Horse Sense 101," as a course, was offered to business, civic leaders, ministers, and social service agency directors in the community.

A sampling of comments from the participants in the course reflect their perceptions of the impact of the information.

Quotes:

"Thank you for seeing a need for this type of training, and bringing it to our community."

"Basic knowledge that is essential in the workplace, especially for supervision."

"Fun, practical, can use it tomorrow!"

"Thank you for offering this—I need it!"

"Very informative, very exciting and lots of good advice."

"Very relevant to me as a manager."

"Fun, informative!"

"I can relate to what we studied—STEWARDS and SERVANTS."

"It is very applicable to my work situations."

"I really did learn and enjoy the sessions. The information affirmed what I have been thinking."

"Eye opener to what constitutes a good leader—STEWARD and SERVANT."

"Provided awareness as to why some leaders display poor leadership qualities, and causes one to avoid that. Very helpful, STEWARD and SERVANT role."

"Great Information!"

"Very relevant to my work situation."

"This was very interesting—I got several ideas."

"Very good training."

"Very applicable information gained!"

"I have enjoyed Horse Sense 101; It has been very informative."

"I learned a lot of practical information that I can put into use."

"This was an excellent class!"

"Class was very worthwhile; It was helpful personally (in personal/family relationship)."

"Thank you Don. I pray I have learned from your wisdom. May all you put your hands to prosper!"